THE POOL OF WISDOM

Includes

WHO BRINGS THE TRUTH
BY WHAT AUTHORITY
and
THREE POEMS

by

J. Krishnamurti

THE BOOK TREE
San Diego, California

© 1928
The Star Publishing Trust
Eerde – Ommen – Holland
Krishnamurti Writings, Inc.
Ojai, CA; London; Madras, India

New material and revisions
© 2014
The Book Tree
All rights reserved
No part of this book may be reproduced, transmitted or utilized in any form or by any means, electronic or mechanical, including photocopying, recording, scanning or by any information storage or retrieval system, without written permission from the publisher, except for brief quotations in articles, books and reviews.

ISBN 978-1-58509-356-4

Cover layout
Mike Sparrow

Cover image copyright
by Damiano Poli

Published by
The Book Tree
P.O. Box 16476
San Diego, CA 92176
www.thebooktree.com

We provide fascinating and educational products to help awaken the public to new ideas and information that would not be available otherwise.
Call 1 (800) 700-8733 for our *FREE BOOK TREE CATALOG*.

CONTENTS

INTRODUCTION, by Paul Tice.......................................5

THE POOL OF WISDOM..7
Ommen Camp fire Talks, 1926

WHO BRINGS THE TRUTH..43
An Address given at Eerde, 1927

BY WHAT AUTHORITY..57
Ommen Camp fire Talks, 1927

THREE POEMS..93
The Simple Union
The Garden of My Heart
Come Away

THE ORDER OF THE STAR......................................100

AFTERWORD..101

INTRODUCTION

This is an early collection of important teachings from Krishnamurti consisting of three talks and three poems.

The Pool of Wisdom is the first talk presented here, given in 1926. It is an in-depth exploration of happiness – what it truly consists of and how one may best identify and obtain it. The reader may come away with a far better understanding of what they must do to know happiness at its fullest extent.

Who Brings the Truth is the second talk presented, given in August of 1927. He explains what it means being in the role of World-Teacher to both himself and for the audience. This may have been the very first talks where, being in the role of a powerful teacher, he shunned his followers. He instead instructed them on how to think for themselves and how to find the true authority that resides within. Otherwise, he tells them, you are just walking blindly through this world. This talk also ties into *The Pool of Wisdom* because it brings the reader back in line with achieving happiness and liberation.

By What Authority is the third talk presented, also given in 1927. Its purpose is to allow each reader to discover his own source of greatness. This talk makes such a thing possible if one can truly hear the message. He tells the story of humanity by using himself as an example, and asks the audience to follow along, using themselves in the same way. It is an amazingly powerful and personal tale that is, by itself, worth the price of the book. It is a brilliant explanation of what authority really is, and where one must go to find it. When you find this authority you also find one of the most sought after things there is – Truth. He explains how, once it is found – truly found – you actually *become* your own Truth. Then, and only then, does liberation and happiness occur, which the first two talks also encompass.

It was just two years after these 1927 talks were given when Krishnamurti dissolved the Order of the Star of the East and walked away from the position of World-Teacher. He did this, officially, through another talk presented to the same general audience at the Ommen Camp in Holland. The reasons given are foretold as clear precursors in this book, which also shed light on Krishnamurti's most significant early teachings. For those who are interested, his final, farewell talk can be found in its entirety in my book entitled *Triumph of the Human Spirit: The Greatest Achievements of the Human Soul and How Its Power can Change Your Life*.

Most anyone who would be placed in the position "the" World-Teacher, and recognized by so many as such, would likely be carried away by their ego and take full advantage of such a lofty recognition. They would feed off the adoration and attention – should they have great wisdom, maybe not to an extravagent degree, but enough to hold onto the position and live an important, self-gratifying life. Krishnamurti, however, cared more about those who were listening than to pursue such ends, as this book will clearly testify.

This book is a great instruction manual for opening the mind and for accessing greater realms of possibility. It will allow the reader to shed their narrow, negative judgments and limitations. Without judgments and limitations, Truth becomes far easier to find.

Paul Tice

THE POOL OF WISDOM
OMMEN CAMP FIRE TALKS, 1926

I

What is the Kingdom of Happiness, where does it exist and how can we attain it? What does it mean, and in what manner can we conquer it? By what thoughts and by what feelings, by what control and by what steady straining, shall we attain that perfection of eternal Happiness, and enter that garden where there are many shadows that give peace, where there is beauty, tranquillity, where there is destruction of the separate self?

I want from the very outset to say that I speak in all humility, though I may perhaps use strong phrases, that I do not want you to obey blindly or listen without thought, that I speak in the sincerity which I feel and that you must listen likewise if you would properly understand. It is, as it were, that I am looking through a larger opening at the same sky that is seen by each one of you. You are perhaps looking through a smaller opening and perceiving only a part of the firmament, while perhaps I may be looking through a wider window which shows me the beauty and glory of that sky. In all friendship, in all sincerity, I invite you to my window and I ask you to quit your small opening, to come and look through a bigger opening at a more beautiful view. In that spirit only do I speak.

I would ask you to look at it, not emotionally, not sentimentally, not mesmerised by words, but with your minds, not to be carried away by mass hypnotism, not to act as one of a crowd, but to use your minds individually and think the problem out for yourselves. Where there are large crowds gathered, we find people all thinking alike; when their feelings are stirred, they are apt to be forced along a particular line laid down by the speaker who is for the moment on the platform. You will be doing a great injury, a great injustice, to yourselves if you do that. If you are carried along by the mass, you will fail to understand even that which is very simple.

The mind is the true ruler, the true helper, the true guide; but the mind is also the destroyer, if misused. The mind, when properly used, should be the guiding force for the majority of us. Though we may not be intellectual giants, we have ordinary intelligence, ordinary perception and the power to balance things. When you use the mind in this manner, you have a tremendous helper, a great power to build, to create. It gives power to direct, to control, as do the reins of a fast-running horse; and for this reason you must use your mind and not be merely emotional, if you would understand the subject that I want to put before you.

It is also the mind that gives us the proper ambition. Most of us are not ambitious — we think it is wrong to be ambitious, unspiritual to be ambitious. I say it is not, if ambition is used rightly. If you use your mind to drive you to your particular goal, along the right path, in the right direction, then that ambition is worth possessing; and that is what I mean when I say that ambition of the right kind should be cultivated by all of us. The right kind of ambition gives power, gives vitality, gives that training which is essential for progress. Ambition which is selfish, which desires to dominate, which desires to shine, which is petty — that ambition is wrong. But the ambition that makes you work unselfishly, that gives you power to help, the will, the determination to bear with anything — that is worth

THE POOL OF WISDOM

possessing. Such an ambition is necessary for growth. It is the greatest force in each one of us, the creator of energy. Such ambition, being unselfish, is spiritual.

To understand gives you a power, a sense of tremendous vitality. It is always necessary, essential and important to understand and not merely to feel. You must use your intelligence from the very beginning, from the very first step of the ladder, from the very lowest slopes of that mountain which we are all going to climb.

My ambition is to gain the Kingdom of Happiness, that Kingdom which must be attained by each one of us, which must be part of us, in which we must dwell eternally. It is not to be found in a particular country, or along the shores of the sea, or in some secluded spot away from humanity, or to be found on a beautiful still evening. Like the generations of old who went out to seek treasures, you must go forth in search of this Happiness. You must apply your mind and your heart to discover this hidden garden, this Kingdom of Happiness, which lies within each one of us.

It is not a Kingdom that lies far off, nor an abode for which we need make a voyage to the ends of the earth. You must find the key that opens all the gates of Heaven, all the gardens of ecstasy; and that key is your own inner Voice, that key is your intuition, and with that key you can enter and live everlastingly in that garden. If you have that Voice, clear, perfect and well-trained — the Voice that is born of many experiences, many sorrows, many ecstasies, many pleasures and many pains — if you have that Voice perfected and cultivated, and if that Voice is the only tyrant that you obey, then that Kingdom of Happiness is within the reach of everyone of you.

As the river dances down to the sea — every rock

THE POOL OF WISDOM

causing the waters to give forth music, every pebble making a new song — at every bend of the shore there is a new enjoyment and at every fall there is a roar. As the river dances down to the sea, enjoying, having ecstasies on its way, it has but one aim, one purpose. Though meandering, it is always sedulously seeking the shortest course to the ocean, to that sea of infinity where there is no individuality, no sense of separation, no sense of solitude and loneliness. Until that river enters into the sea, it is always an individual stream, having its own ecstasies, its own troubles, its own songs. As the river, so must you be.

As the tremendous roar of a great river is enticing, beautiful and magnificent, so is the Voice of him who is struggling towards that sea of Infinity, of Nirvana, of Moksha, of Heaven, where there is no separate self. Though you may have many experiences in going towards the sea, for you must have experiences, you, like the river, should have but one thought, one purpose, one determination—to reach that vast ocean.

So each one of us must seek, so each one of us must dance through life, must have tremendous ecstasies, great sorrows and pains and great pleasures; and the greater and stronger they are, the more quickly shall we arrive at that stage of Nirvana, that absolute oneness with Life.

When once you have drunk at the fountain of all knowledge, of all wisdom, which is Happiness, nothing else in the world will ever satisfy you. Every one who is struggling, who is living, who is dancing through life, has that Happiness in store for him. But every one who seeks that Happiness must obey that Voice whose dominion, whose power, whose authority he alone can recognise.

THE POOL OF WISDOM

For many years I have searched for that Happiness, I have wandered through many climes, I have read many books, I have perhaps suffered a little; but I have always desired that Vision, that Happiness, which no pleasures of this earth can ever give. And for some months past, I have found it; for some months past I have lived in that Kingdom and that Kingdom has become real.

For this reason, I would have you breathe that scented air, that air of divinity, that scent of perfection. I would urge you to come with me, and would make you enjoy and sport yourselves in the shadows of that garden, and then it will not matter what you are, whether you are a Sannyasi — the man who has given up the world — or whether you have great possessions and live in a palace. You are then detached from everything, but you are at the same time interested in all things.

For this reason, it is important, essential that you should understand with your mind. It is so easy to weep, so easy to cry, so easy to be emotional over such things, but if you once understand with your mind, it gives you the strength to guide yourself. You are the Absolute, you are the Path, you are in every tree in that garden, in every plant, in every creature.

If you would understand, you must obey only that Voice within each one of you. If you would see that Vision, you must obey that Voice, absolutely and completely. But you must take care that that Voice is the Real Voice, that has become purified and ennobled through great experiences, great sorrows, great pains and great pleasures. That Voice will have such power, such dominion, such authority over you, that you can but obey its commands. And then you will enter that garden, enter that Kingdom of Happiness; and when once you have tasted its delights, when once you have seen the vision within, you need not be held down by anything on earth, you are at the source of eternal Happiness.

I would make you all come to know my Happiness, take you all with me to that garden, show you that vision, make you see the glory and perfection of it, and when once you have walked in that garden, you will have the power, the authority to bring others to it.

You will then not only receive, but have the power to give.

II

All wise people, all people who are searching after knowledge, must look about them and contemplate. All things, whether living or non-living, are transient. Nothing is lasting, nothing is permanent. There is birth and death; there is a rush and a jostle; there is a passing pain and a passing joy; there are cravings, unsatisfied desires, desires that can never be satisfied; there is an immense ocean of nothingness. Affections and love fade as the delicate flower of a secluded valley; there is rejoicing at birth, and sorrow at death. A day of glory is as a passing cloud. All things, whether living or non-living, are subject to decay and they perish; all go down to the grave, and hence to the dust.

Wherever we look, there is this chaos, this vast unrest, this something that cannot be satisfied. And the contemplative mind that seeks the reason of things must ask, must demand, must search out and find if there is anything lasting, anything permanent, anything enduring, any resting-place.

Is there not an abode where we can be free from

THE POOL OF WISDOM

desires, from those desires that are unsatisfiable, where the mind can be tranquil, peaceful and composed? Is there no Eternity where nothing changes, nothing decays, nothing can fade? The wise mind contemplates, looks around, sees these transient things, and then asks: Is there not something that will last, something which is Eternal?

Those, who have not found that Eternity, cannot answer; and those, who have found it, can but answer vaguely, for each must find that which he seeks according to his evolution, according to his stage of thought and of feeling. But we can all have the same vision, we can see the same beauty, though our lips may translate it into words which convey different meanings.

Those who are wise, those who are full of age — not necessarily of the body, but full of age that comes through experience, through many sorrows, through many pains, through many pleasures and through many ecstasies — those can say, if they have once seen that vision, that there is Eternity, that it is beyond the possibility of doubt.

What then is this Vision? It is Truth. Truth is permanent, everlasting. It has no beginning and no end, it is changeless and immortal. And when you ask: "Where does it abide, where can I find it?" — I say: "You will find it only in that Kingdom of Happiness."

If you would find it, you must apply your mind and your heart to know, to seek, and to search out that Pool of Heaven which is Wisdom, which is Truth. For there, in that Kingdom, in the Holy of Holies, we must learn, we must experience, we must grow mentally and emotionally, and find that image which is the incarnation, which is the embodiment of Truth, which is Eternal. And like

THE POOL OF WISDOM

all people who are not satisfied by the mere world of passing glories that this can give, by the flatteries of friends, you must seek, must brush aside the undergrowth in the forest, if you would see the clear skies of heaven. You must cut away the dead branches of life, before you can see the stars by which you can guide your way out of the forest of transient things.

In such a way must we set about it. In such a way I set about it. I saw my Eternity. I saw the source of all things, the beauty, the perfection, and the joy of all things. I tasted Immortality. What I saw can be described only from my point of view, can be given only in words that may seem to mean very little. But when you have longed for it and it has come; when once you have seen it for yourself, when once it is the very breath of your life, then you will understand, then you will know that you have tasted Immortality, that you have seen the permanent, the lasting and unchangeable.

There is nothing in the world that can give satisfaction, that can satisfy your cravings, except that Immortality, that finding of Truth. But he who would seek that Pool of Wisdom, that Kingdom of Happiness where Truth abides, must first learn to destroy self. He must first learn to appreciate and to feel the greatness of real friendship, the friendship that comes when you feel one with all things, when you have no existence apart from others; when in everything about you, through the transient, you see the Eternal; when every word, when every person, when every passing cloud and all things of earth give a new meaning, have a different song, a different pleasure, and a different Happiness. Then you will be able to enter into that Kingdom of Happiness, where there is the freshness of many breezes.

THE POOL OF WISDOM

For self and Truth cannot exist together. The path of the self leads to sorrow, to pain, and to those fleeting pleasures which we call life, which we take for reality and for the permanent. But Truth leads to the Kingdom of Happiness, because there is forgetfulness of self—that absolute oneness of life, both mental and emotional, which makes you feel and think that you are part of all the world, whether moving or non-moving, whether active or inactive.

But he who would walk to that Kingdom of Happiness, if he would be great, must learn to sacrifice the self, however difficult, however impossible it may be for the moment, however wearying, however painful. He must sacrifice it in order to gain and give greater pleasures, greater Happiness, greater ecstasy, and greater glory, which are lasting.

Since it has been my dream, since it has been my Happiness, since it has been my delight to see that Kingdom, to breathe those scented airs, let us walk there together, let us see it together, and let us explore it together.

Before you can see it with my eyes, before you can think of it through my mind, before you can feel it through my heart, you must have the capacity, you must have the strength, to shatter all prejudices. For what we perceive, shall be the essence of intelligence, the essence of thought, the essence of all emotions, the essence of devotion, the essence of love. And those of us who are prejudiced, those of us who are trammelled, cannot see it in all its beauty, in all its greatness, in all its nobility. For prejudice distorts the vision, as coloured glasses dim the sunshine of the world.

For this reason, those of you who would see it as it

should be seen, who would see it as it is, must come freely and fearlessly, exultant and controlled. But you must have obeyed the Voice within to arrive at that growth; and having for the moment shattered those walls of prejudice, those narrow limits that bind you, let us examine it, let our minds — and not only our hearts — examine it.

When you see a statue, which is the perfection of human art, or a fair vision of the mountain top in the light of the evening sun, or the sheen on the wing of a fast-flying bird, or a lovely flower in the field, or a strong tree set apart — when you have seen such physical glory, and when you can retain that vision and keep it, and make use of it at those times when you have tumultuous emotions both of depression and of great ecstasy, and when that vision can give you Happiness, satisfy your fleeting disturbances with its physical appearances of beauty, of divinity, and of pleasure — it shows that the mind and the heart can react to that for which each one of us is craving, for which each one of us is asking.

Likewise the Vision of Eternity, this Truth. You must live with it. Every moment that you are not occupied with the fleeting, that you are not taking pleasure in the passing — that very moment you must dwell with that beauty, take it and keep it as a precious jewel. If you have seen the ordinary, physical vision of beauty, it often recurs in moments of trouble. It is the feeble mind and the weak heart that soon forget the beauty of it, and so eventually forget that beauty which is lasting and that Happiness which is permanent.

If we are wise, if we have a heart that is not prejudiced and a mind that is pure, then the physical vision of great beauty always remains. You can always go back and

THE POOL OF WISDOM

live in it, and you can forget the outer world. You can always breathe that air which is ecstatic. And likewise, when once you have seen this Kingdom of Happiness, this garden of many roses, this abode of ecstasy and immortality, when once you have grasped it with a pure mind and a clean heart, then you can always live in that Kingdom. And then from that reality you can go back and wander forth into the unreal, from the real to the unreal; whereas most of us live in the unreal and wander seldom in the real.

It is always the transient things which we take as the reality; and for this reason, that vision of greatness, that vision of nobility, is rare because we are surrounded, dominated, by passing things. For this reason, it is much more difficult for a mind and for a heart that is not peaceful, that is not quiet, that is always agitated, to retain that vision which it has once seen—which every one of us has seen, since to see it is not the exception.

Every one of us has seen the beauty of the sunset, of a tree, of the fast-flying bird in a still sky. *There* is the reality, if you would see the Happiness through the unreal, if you would see the Truth which is transcendent. But you must have eyes, eyes that have long been accustomed to visions of beauty, that are capable of long search, capable of retaining what they have seen, whatever be the troubles, whatever be the sorrows, whatever be the pain.

When once you have entered into that Holy of Holies which is Truth, then you need not lose it again, because you are part of Eternity. Then no glory of earth, then no personal friends, passing love, nor any of those things matter; for you belong to that Eternity, for you have drunk at that Pool of Heaven which is wisdom.

THE POOL OF WISDOM

When once you have entered it, you can always go forth and see the fleeting things of the world. Then only can you give Happiness and sympathy. Then only can you give those realities which are lasting.

You must of your own accord enter that Kingdom, that garden, that abode of Truth which is Happiness. Of your own strength, of your own desire, of your own greatness, must you create this greatness which is everlasting. Of your own perfection, of your own genius, must you create this immortality. For what I create, or anyone else creates, can only be the passing; but what you yourself create through your own experience, is lasting, is permanent.

When you enter that Kingdom, then you begin to understand that the self, the giver of sorrow and pain and all the fierce physical pleasures, has no control over you, has no sway over you — that its dominion and its power have weakened.

As you grow into that perfection, and enter into that Holy of Holies where abides Truth, more and more you cease to exist as a separate being. This is the only Truth, this is the only spirituality, this is the only Happiness that any human being can find.

III

Most of us here, in all sincerity, are looking for the Great Teacher; we are looking for Him whom we love, who is the Source of all things, the Source of perfection, the Source of beauty.

That being the case, we shall naturally look to that perfection, we shall naturally look to that beauty, and we must finish with those external phenomena, those

THE POOL OF WISDOM

things by which we are mesmerised, those phrases, those labels that we invent. We must set aside these things.

I should like to put before you my point of view; I should like you to reason it out, and, if you think it right, follow it according to your best and highest capacity and your purest intuition.

My point is this. You have studied for many years, and have learnt through many books that you have temperaments, that you are separate types of individuals — different from others and myself — and you have learnt that you have your own particular rôle to play in life. Now during all these years you have been trying to fulfil that rôle which you have found for yourselves. You have been walking either firmly or weakly, either with your head high or with halting footsteps along the path, which you thought the highest, along the path, which you thought would lead to nobility, to beauty, to perfection.

Now a time must come when you ask yourself: What have I done with all that knowledge, with all the labels, with all the phrases and all the jargons I have learned? In what way have I created, in what way have I given, and brought joy to those people who suffer and are longing and desirous to learn, those people who are fumbling in the darkness?

What have you, with your phrases, with your labels, with your books, achieved?

How many people have you made happy, not in the passing things, but in the ways of the Eternal?

Have you given the Happiness that lasts, the Happiness that is never failing, the Happiness that cannot be dimmed by a passing cloud?

You must ask yourself what you have done.

THE POOL OF WISDOM

In what way have you created a protecting wall, so that people shall not slip into pitfalls?
How far have you built a railing along that deep river into which every human being is liable to fall?
How far have you helped those people who want to climb?
How far has it been your ambition to lead someone to that Kingdom of Happiness, that garden where there is unchanging light, unchanging beauty?
You must question yourself; you must reason with yourself, as I have questioned and reasoned with myself.
We invent phrases to satisfy ourselves.
And with all that you have at your disposal, with all these things which you think are really vital and important, what have you done?
In what manner have you brought forth that precious jewel, so that it shall shine and guide the whole world?
In what way have you given, in what way have you grown, and in what way have you led others?
It is very gratifying and very satisfying to call ourselves by different names and different types, and to segregate ourselves, and to think that we are different from the rest of the world.
But, if you are all these things, have you saved one from sorrow?
Have any of you given me Happiness — "me" the ordinary person?
Have any of you saved me sorrow?
Have any of you given me the nourishment of heaven when I was hungry?
Have any of you felt so deeply that you could throw yourself into the place of the person who is suffering?
What have you produced, what have you brought forth?

THE POOL OF WISDOM

What is your work?
Why should you be different because you belong to different societies, different sects, have different temperaments?
In what are you different from myself?
What is your work and what is your purpose?
What have you done with your days?
In what way have you fulfilled those things that are given, and in what condition and in what manner do you hold yourself?
And what has it all meant to each one of you?
And now myself, being an ordinary person, I would ask you to look at my point of view; I would ask you to come and look through my window, which will show you my heaven, which will show you my garden and my abode.
Then you will see that what matters is not what you do, what you read, what any person says you are or are not, but that you should have the intense desire to enter into that abode where dwells Truth.
Because there lies true Happiness, there is the only Kingdom worth possessing — not in useless phrases.
And I would have you come and see it; I would have you come and feel it; I would have you come, and think, and ponder over it, and not say to me: "Oh, you are different, you are on the mountain top, you are a mystic."
You give me phrases and cover my Truth with your words.
I do not want you to break with all that you believe.
I do not want you to deny your temperament.
I do not want you to do things that you do not feel to be right.

THE POOL OF WISDOM

But, are any among you happy?
Have you, any of you, tasted Eternity?
Do you know what Immortality is, what Truth is? By that only can you be judged and by nothing else.
Do not invent phrases; do not cover the Truth by things that are not real, that have no purpose, no vitality, that do not give you strength and ecstasy of purpose.
I say, if you come to that Kingdom and live and abide there, then you will possess the spark of the genius, then you will belong to those who are the true builders, who give Happiness to the world. Then you are giving, you are producing, and whatever you do will bear the mark of the creator.
I say that I am on firmer ground, on more beautiful ground, with greater strength, greater glory, than those who are in the bog, than those who think that, because it is so difficult to break all the things that they have created, it is very difficult to reach my Kingdom, that it is very difficult to come there.
But surely, if you were in the bog, you would not hesitate to step on firmer ground where there is sunshine, freshness and pure air.
You must choose.
What does temperament, what do titles matter, if you have entered that Kingdom which is the source of Truth, the source of Eternity, where you cease to be as a separate self?
Why should you hesitate to come and see? I do not ask you to follow me; but I ask you to come and look at those things that are real, that are permanent.
I would ask you, as members of the Star, who believe in the Coming, who know what it means to breathe the same air as He does, who know what it means to look

THE POOL OF WISDOM

at the same sunshine as He does, who enjoy the same flower as He does, I would ask you: Are you going to make Him bend to your temperament, make Him believe all the things that you believe? Are you going to persuade Him that your path is the best path? Because if you are going to do that, you will find that you have lost the glory, that you have lost the precious jewel, that the sun has set for you, nor will there be another sunrise.

Every one of you is frightened, because you dare not come out of your little path, your little window, and walk with Him. You want Him to walk with you, with your ideas, your idiosyncrasies and your particular fancies.

But a time must come — and it is coming, nearer and nearer than you realise, happier and happier than you can conceive — a time is coming when you must choose. We have used these words thousands and thousands of times but they have not meant anything. Now the time has come when you must choose whether you are going to follow Him, to breathe the same air, to climb the same mountain, along the same path, or whether you are going to try to bend Him to your particular will, to your particular temperament, to your particular prejudices.
That will not be.
Because I belong to all people, to all who really love, to all who are suffering.
And if you would walk, you must walk with me.
If you would understand, you must look through my mind.
If you would feel, you must look through my heart.
And because I really love, I want you to love.
Because I really feel, I want you to feel.
Because I hold everything dear, I want you to hold all things dear.

THE POOL OF WISDOM

Because I want to protect, you should protect.
And this is the only life worth living, and the only Happiness worth possessing.

IV

You have been listening to me for the last two or three evenings and you have been willing to look at the world through my eyes. Because I have really been feeling and thinking very deeply for some time, and because I feel tremendous affection — sincere and honest affection — for most people here, I should like to take you once more, take you as often as I can, to that place where I found my Happiness, where I found my Truth.

But in so doing, I should like to give you my personal experience — not that I want your salutations or your respect — but because, perhaps, it might help and might give you a distinct idea of what I have in mind.

Some months ago, when I was in the hills, away from people, where there were many woods and many streams, I remember one day walking with a friend, and saying to him: "What a nice place this is in which to meditate." It happened that he went away, leaving me alone for a minute, and I casually turned round, admiring the archway which the trees formed, and then — all of a sudden — I saw my Happiness, my Guru, my Teacher, the Teacher of every one of us, walking towards me. It seemed to me that I looked through Him at all things, through Him at all trees, and I stood there gazing, and astonished that I should see such a wonder, such magnificence and such glory quite unexpectedly, not at that moment yearning for Him to appear. But nevertheless He was there, and as I went to my room He went with

THE POOL OF WISDOM

me, always leading, looking at me, going down that narrow path which led to my room.

Ever since then it has been my Happiness, my intense joy to see all things through Him, to see trees, human beings, skies, all in Him. If I saw a little thing, an ant or a blade of grass, or the fish in the pond, He filled it and I looked at it through Him. And having such intense Happiness in possessing such a jewel, in entertaining eternally such a Companion, I felt that I must sing, that I must share, that I must make others understand. That is one of the most difficult things — to make others understand and see Him, to make them realise that He is not something outside themselves, something far away, but that He is wherever there is a clean heart, wherever there is a pure mind, and wherever there have been countless disappointments and innumerable sorrows and troubles and immense joy.

Possessing such precious ointment that shall still the many pains, the other night I lay awake thinking in what manner I could bring that Happiness to others, in what way I could convince them that there is only one Temple, one Church, one Light-bringer, one Law-giver, one Truth. In what way could we all arrive at the same place, even though we may walk by different routes, even though some of us may have to use stepping-stones, some on crutches, some with bleeding feet, some with perfect bodies and choosing a shorter path? We must all eventually come where He shall be our eternal Companion; where there shall be no parting, no separation; where there is no sense of loneliness; where there is no unhappiness.

I want to make you realise, to give you enough strength, to give you enough understanding to see the

THE POOL OF WISDOM

mighty things that are about you for yourselves. What you see and what you have and what you possess is your own. Nobody can take it away; nobody can wrest that precious thing from you. You can never again doubt, you can never again feel that you are alone and struggling by yourself, for you have with you Him, for whom the whole world longs, as your friendly Companion who accompanies you wherever you go, as a Friend to whom you can talk, as a God at whose feet you can worship. You do not desire to possess Him for yourself alone, you want to share Him with others. It is the same with Truth. If you love Truth intensely and yet absolutely for its own sake, you love all. If Truth is the one comfort, and you have that comfort, your desire is to share it with others.

That has been my glory, that has been my Happiness. I have found that which I have desired, that for which I have longed, the one Truth and the one Altar, where I can kneel and know that I am there for Eternity, with certainty that nobody can take my glory from me.

For this reason I wish I could give each one of you the power, the strength to see these things for yourselves. I can give you the inspiration, because it is easier for me, having conquered it, to share it with others, but those who have not partaken, cannot partake of it with others. Since I have tasted it, I naturally desire to share it — the Kingdom of Happiness — the only Truth worth possessing. In that abode you can forget yourself, your troubles, your sorrows, for all things are in Him.

We are as fish caught in an evil net of transient things. But if you yourself are the fisherman, if you yourself are the fish, and if you yourself are the net and the water, then the world of sorrow — the world that creates

THE POOL OF WISDOM

sorrow, pain and fleeting pleasures — ceases to be because you have that which is Eternal.

I felt one day that I had lost that which I thought I had found for Eternity. It was a very good experience, because you must if you would grow, have those things which you cling to, taken away from you for a moment. For some hours I had lost my precious jewel and I cannot tell you how I felt — I was half suffocating, half crying inside, I was going through all the agonies of having lost something which I had once held, I was dazed, I was in a state of Maya, in a state where one sees nothing but confusion. Then I went out to find Him whom my soul adores. Suddenly, as I went along, He appeared in front of a tree and I saw that tree through Him. It was worth losing Him — that little darkness of a few hours — to find Him again, to find that Kingdom of Happiness, that Truth again. Since then I always have Him with me. And living, possessing, and having my being in Him, I wish, like every one in the world who possesses something really precious, to share with all. But I do not desire you to see the same thing I see, for you must perceive the glory through your own eyes, see the beauty of Him and feel His glory through your own hearts. And then what you have and what you possess and what you have created is your own. I tell you, because I know, and because that is the only thing worth possessing. I should like you to come and see my Heaven, my part of that garden, and then, when once you have been there, once you have really enjoyed those cool shades of Eternity, then you will find that whatever happens, whatever shadow is passing, leaves no mark. But you leave an imprint on the world, as you give to the world instead of receiving, as you build

THE POOL OF WISDOM

instead of destroying, as you protect instead of killing.

I would make all of you drink at my fountain, I would make all of you breathe that scented air, so that you can yourselves become creators, geniuses, who make the world happy. If you possess that Kingdom, you do not desire the world. You are the essence of spirituality, you are the personification of Him, and you are always the comforter and the protector of the world.

For this reason you must awaken, you must walk along with me and follow. I should like you to feel the glory for yourselves, to perceive the beauty for yourselves, and to acquire the precious thing for yourselves. And then, when you have found it, you can make people see the reality, make people feel that you are the reality and that they can become part of it.

Do you not see that then all quarrels cease, that all sects, all temperaments, become unified? You are with Him and He is in you. Wherever you go, into whatever climes you wander, you bring comfort, you bring Happiness and enlightenment to those that suffer.

Therefore I would take you into my garden, I would invite you to my abode, I would lead you into that Kingdom of Happiness. Like men of experience, who have suffered and had pleasures and pains, you must walk; whether you walk on your crutches, whether you walk bare-foot, it does not much matter so long as you get there. Whether you take one path or another does not much matter, since all lead to the same Kingdom of Happiness.

When you do not understand, it is so difficult to make you feel and realise that it is a certainty and not a dream of mine, not a passing thing that I have invented, with which to entice you.

THE POOL OF WISDOM

But if it be imagination, is it not worth possessing such an imagination, is it not worth creating such imagery? But it is not imagination, it is not a passing thing, it is not an invention. You cannot invent such things, you cannot imagine such things, for this Kingdom is real, it is the abode of unchanging Truth.

You, who are all longing, seeking, searching, applying your minds and hearts to find this, I ask you to come and enjoy, to be really happy in all the things that you do, even though you are suffering. I have found it, and if one person can find it, thousands and millions of others will find it.

That is the only Truth, the only Altar, the only Temple where you can worship, where you can be with Eternity, where you can know Immortality. And then you become the real Teacher, you become the Redeemer of mankind, you become the World Lover. When you feel strongly and think strongly of the Reality, and live for that Reality, and keep your heart clean for that Reality, then you are in the Kingdom of Happiness, and you wander forth and give your blessing to the world that needs it.

For this reason I desire, if I can, to exchange with you. You can take all of me; you can take my heart, my mind, everything away from me, enjoy of it, eat of it, because I can always find it again, having once found it. It is the blind who are in need, not those who have already seen, who have plenty. You have not plenty, I have. You have so little, I have so much. You need, and I have more than sufficient. Why not exchange? Why not look at the world through the eyes of Reality? Why not feel the suffering of the world through the heart that is Eternal?

THE POOL OF WISDOM

When once you look and feel, you can do nothing else but work, nothing else but love. And when you work and love, combining with that Truth, which is the absolute, the forgetting of self, you become the real disciple, the real follower, the real lover.

Before understanding, you must have this desire to be a part of Him, to be like Him, and to be as the beautiful flower in the field.

Then every word that I shall speak, you will understand; my every whisper you shall hear.

V

There is a lingering thought of depression, a little touch of sadness, that each of us feels when we depart from those we like. It is natural and it is human.

We have all of us, I think, been for a while in that scented garden, enjoyed its shades and been happy. We have known what it is to be really happy. We have tasted that Happiness. Even though it were for a brief moment, we have lived in that delight, in that ecstasy, in that serious joyousness, which comes when we really dwell in that abode.

When once we have tasted of that fountain of Wisdom, when we have listened to that voice of Truth, all things — sorrows and pains, such as we feel when we part — disappear, because each minute and each second, every day and every year, we are creating that garden around us, wherever we may be. We are giving to others that beauty, and we are sharing with others that nectar of the Gods.

When once we have enjoyed that Kingdom, we must share that Happiness with others. We must realise that

THE POOL OF WISDOM

there is only one Truth, one Abode. When we have really and sincerely felt it, the sense of separation, the sense of loneliness, the sense of being different from others, truly vanishes. And when such a thing does happen, as it does to a few people of the world, then they become the standard for the world, the standard by which we compare, the standard to which the world looks.

I should like, when we separate, that each one of you take with you that Happiness in your different ways and by different means. Either you can guard it and keep it for yourself, or, as the perfume-seller, who really enjoys the perfume, take it out and give it to others. Ask them to share in it, to delight in the perfume, which you have gathered. But you must first gather it, if you would share it with others.

I have felt an immense desire that you should take away with you the Kingdom of Happiness, that you should know this Happiness, whether it be of your imagination or whether it be of mine.

As long as you have this Happiness within you, as long as you have felt that Truth within you, as long as there is that repose and tranquillity, then you have, in truth, tasted and enjoyed that Pool of Heaven which is Wisdom.

Even though we cannot all at the same time taste the same thing in the same way, yet there is the certainty that we shall all drink at the same fountain.

We must develop a wise passiveness, a wise tranquillity, a wise repose. Wise passiveness does not mean stagnation, for while waiting you can prepare the ground. As the labourer prepares the earth, so must you prepare your garden. Pull out all the little weeds, remove all the little stones that spoil your garden and make it ugly. Destroy all those things that do not produce, kill out all those things that hinder the growth of the flower, annihilate the ugliness, the pettiness, the trivialities that exist in such gardens as are created by a small soul. If you can do this, then you will develop a wise passiveness.

When the song is sung, when the real voice of Truth has spoken, you will have within you the responsive soul and that responsive voice, so that we can all sing together, so that our song can fill the air, so that our song can fill the hearts of men.

When we have sung such a song, when we have felt such a Truth together, then there is no separation, then there is no idea that you are giving and I am taking, or that I am giving and you are taking. We all live in that garden, we all feel alike; and how then can there be any separation, any idea that we are different from each other? And this sense, this quality of wise passiveness — if I may so call it — gives a different tone, a fresh breath, and a new understanding.

Because you possess this passiveness, this tranquillity, whatever is done to you — whatever wrong, whatever hurt, whatever mischief — you will develop your heart and your mind along the right path. You do not harden, grow bitter, or become suppressed.

For us, however different we may be, however wise we may be, and however small or big we may be, in that garden there is no comparison, there is no difference, nor is there that struggle born of individuality, because we have lost that sense of separateness. As long as we hear that music, as long as we are all breathing that scented air, we forget, we lose the illusion that our own self is much more important than another's.

THE POOL OF WISDOM

You must become joy-intoxicated, you must become God-like, in this garden.

You must then come into this Garden of Happiness, into this Kingdom where there is Truth, where there is Eternity. When once you have entered it, you can always go forth, you can always return.

Even though there be sorrow, even though there be pain, you can always have within you that bubbling spring of well-being, of contentment born of divine discontent. You can be the bringer of Truth to those who have not tasted those ecstasies that are found on the heights.

We must develop naturally — neither struggle nor strive unnaturally. As long as we possess the inner Voice, all the qualities which we think we should have, and for which we are struggling, will come naturally.

People worry over their misfortunes, their little angers, little sins. It does not matter, for they have no value if there is this inner sense of greatness, of beauty, of perfection. If you possess that absolutely, nothing in the world can shake your foundations. You can build storey upon storey, you can climb nearer and nearer to the stars and the sky, but you can never be shaken and your foundation will never weaken.

You must enter this Kingdom, you must drink at this Pool of Heaven, you must all come to my garden, you must all cast away your ignorance, your little knowledge, when you enter this garden. Those things that you consider important, those things that you hold as of value, have no reality, cannot exist there.

If you prepare wisely, if you consider, and if you give thought, then you will hear this song eternally. You will live eternally with Him, you will be His eternal companion.

THE POOL OF WISDOM

Do you not see that it makes life much more beautiful, gives a freshness, a tranquillity, to every moment of the day? Such a Kingdom and the conquering of it is worth all struggles, all pains and all joys.

We must go out and sing this song to those who have not heard it, who unfortunately have not ears to hear it. In order to do so, you must come into this garden; you must gather with full arms the flowers in it; you must take them out and give. You cannot help giving when you possess. It is because you do not possess that you do not know how to give. Once you have, you can always give.

Let us all go to those heights where there is perfection, where there is beauty, where there is the sense of oneness, of being really friendly, really affectionate. Then you do not worry about anything in life, then you do not struggle, then you do not suffer pain — though these things have a meaning, they drop off like the drop of water from the lotus leaf. Like the lotus, you develop from impurity, and come out of the mire into freshness, into cleanliness, into beauty. Such is the Kingdom of Happiness.

But you must have the Voice, that pure Voice which will lead you, that true intuition which will guide you. And when you have that, then you yourself become part of Him, then in yourself is His abode.

There lies the beauty of your whole life, there lies the whole vision. And you do not want greater Kingdoms to conquer.

When once you have Him, and when once He speaks, when once He looks through your eyes, you know what it means when the wind sings through every tree, when every star shines and every human being loves.

THE POOL OF WISDOM

You are everything, and He is in you.

Therefore I would urge you, I would beg you to come. I would exchange, if I could, my heart, my mind, for yours, because I have this and some of you have it not.

When once you have it, you want to share; because then you cannot see or tolerate sorrow or pain in others. This desire is a natural thing, a beautiful thing, nothing supernatural, nothing extraordinary. Because you are the source of things, because you are the creator of things, you want to alter, to create, to make those things that are ugly, beautiful, those people that are unhappy, happy.

For this reason it is worth while to climb, worth while to struggle and to attain the Kingdom of Happiness.

You must come into that Garden, you must live there eternally, you must feel, grope, struggle incessantly, until you are there. And then you cease to struggle, then you exist like a flower in the sunshine, giving forth beauty, comfort and scent to all the passers-by.

For this reason, He comes to teach you how to attain that Kingdom of Happiness.

The feeling of separateness, the feeling of being different, does not exist. What does matter is that all should be happy, all should taste of this fountain. Such is the ideal, such is the Kingdom.

I often feel that we are not sufficiently joyous within ourselves. We are burdened by so many things in life — by our families, by our friends, by our worries, and by our passing thoughts. When once you have unlocked the gate that leads to the Kingdom of Happiness, then all those little things fade away. You do not worry about virtues, you do not worry about sin, you are there in the centre of light, at the source of Happiness, you are there to bring and to give comfort.

THE POOL OF WISDOM

VI

I wonder — if I may be permitted to be quite personal — how much each one of you has really gained, how much each one of you has accumulated during our Camp, now that we have time to think, to look around and to consider.

For myself, I have learnt considerably. I have learnt to be really excited, in the proper sense, in the nicest possible way; because you must be excited to do things, you must be intense to do things; and with the excitement you must have the opposite, you must have repose, you must have the training to keep that excitement under control.

I have really learnt one thing: that is, not to rely on any human being. You will not misunderstand me, for there is nothing wonderful about it; but, for your spiritual, for your mental, for your emotional well-being, you must be detached. If you want to create, if you want to think out, if you want to feel intensely, you must be disinterested, you must cut yourself away from your own personal and narrow affections, from everything that binds; then you are able to judge, then you are able to look at and feel things in their proper proportions.

To give an instance: I remember once, when I was standing in the railway station at Benares (the holy city of India), seeing a Sannyasi, a person who has given up the world, who has adopted the robe of enlightenment, and who carries in his hands the bowl of Happiness. And there were we, a few of us, with numbers of people around; and there was the Sannyasi, a short distance away, very dignified, very calm, with a kind of cold look in his eyes — not hard — but as though he thought:

THE POOL OF WISDOM

"What are all these people doing with their garlands, with their achkans*, with all their possessions?" There he was with his loin cloth, his staff in his hand, and he looked so happy, and he *was* happy, able to judge everything around him from that disinterested point of view. The world could give him nothing, because when a man gives up the world, he has true contentment — not the contentment of stagnation. So he was able to detach himself entirely from all little things. And I have learnt to do that, during all these days of excitement and energy and work.

When you do have some measure of detachment, however little, you enjoy life much more. The things that we experience are as garments for our adornment that we put on or take off without being identified with them. And that is the first thing I have learnt.

I am putting all this before you to help and encourage you to find out for yourselves how you respond to events and whether they have left a mark, deep or superficial, after the experience. You need not tell everyone, but you should ponder over it for yourselves.

You should think out for yourselves what you have gained, what has been the outcome of all these events; for every little thing, every little action, every little thought, if it is properly used, has a great effect if you consider it afterwards. You, then, really become a different person every day.

I myself have altered so much during this fortnight, within and without — my body, my face, my hands, my entire being have changed. That is the only way to

---

* An Indian Coat.

THE POOL OF WISDOM

breathe the fresh air of life — by this constant change, constant turmoil, constant unrest.

That is what makes the difference between the genius and the small man. The genius has a volcano always inside, creating trouble and shooting forth flames into the heavens; whereas the small man is just going along calmly without producing those flames, without shooting those stars into the skies.

If there is this tremendous unrest, you are always searching, you are always willing to learn from the highest as well as from the meanest thing of the earth. We are too apt to look for the great things of life only among the tall trees. That is the second thing I have learnt.

The third thing that I have learnt concerns love. What we call love — human love, human friendship — is a vital thing. You must have human love; but there is a further stage, where you walk over the threshold of this human love into the kingdom of divine love.

Then you can feel that, even though you may be surrounded by thousands of people you like and who like you even though you may be surrounded by many more thousands who are indifferent to you, or even dislike you, it leaves you untouched. You may have superficial disturbances; the lake may be ruffled by the passing winds; but go deeper into the water, and you will find there is the solidity of depth and of great peace.

You are a different person when you have entered into that realm of love, and that is what we all desire. We all crave affection — I as much as anyone else. If we show a little affection to others, we see at once a real joy on their faces. But it is only a stepping stone into that Kingdom of Divinity where you are yourself love.

THE POOL OF WISDOM

When you have grown to that stature, it does not affect you whether anyone likes you or not, whether someone loves you or loves another, for you are the essence of love.

I often imagine that a beautiful great mountain, though it might like admiration, though it might like human appreciation, is always great; whether we admire it or not, it is always beautiful. It must be exactly the same thing with us. We feel lonely, we feel depressed; from those things we must escape.

The fourth thing that I have learnt is observation and adaptability. Through observation you learn; through observation comes adaptability.

One more thing I should like to add. We, who have all been at this Camp, have lived close to Nature, in close proximity to the skies and the stars and all the great things of the world. Do not go back and do small things, do not demean yourselves; be on your guard! It is really easier to do big things than small. If you must fall, fall out of the thirty-third floor, do not stumble on the pavement.

I assure you, you will find real joy in life through this Vision of eternal happiness. To me life is much more beautiful now than ever before, because I have this Happiness within me continually — I am knocking, knocking against doors that are closed and that I desire to open.

If you have that Happiness, you do not want anything else in life. You are absolutely independent. You are happy without the complications which ordinary happiness brings. In you is the source of all happiness.

WHO BRINGS THE TRUTH

AN ADDRESS DELIVERED AT EERDE, OMMEN, HOLLAND, THE INTERNATIONAL HEADQUARTERS OF THE ORDER OF THE STAR, AUGUST 2, 1927

WHO BRINGS THE TRUTH

When I began to think for myself, which has been now for some years past, I found myself in revolt. I was not satisfied by any teachings, by any authority. I wanted to find out for myself what the World-Teacher meant to me and what the Truth was behind the form of the World-Teacher. Before I began to think for myself, before I had the capacity to think for myself, I took it for granted that I, Krishnamurti, was the vehicle of the World-Teacher because many people maintained that it was so. But when I began to think, I wanted to find out what was meant by the World-Teacher, what was meant by the taking of a vehicle by the World-Teacher, and what was meant by His manifestation in the world.

I am going to be purposely vague, because although I could quite easily make it definite, it is not my intention to do so. Because once you define a thing it becomes dead. If you make a thing definite — at least that is what I maintain — you are trying to give an interpretation which in the minds of others will take a definite form and hence they will be bound by that form from which they will have to liberate themselves.

What I am going to tell you is not on authority, and you must not obey, but understand. It is not a question of authority, nor of set lines which you must follow blindly — that is what most of you are wanting. You want me to lay down the law, you want me to say: I am so and so; so that you can say: all right, we will work for you. That is not the reason why I am explaining, but it is in order that we should understand each other, that we should help each other. I would make you see

WHO BRINGS THE TRUTH

things now which you may see for yourselves, perhaps in this life or in some future life.

Now, when I was a small boy I used to see Shri Krishna, with the flute, as He is pictured by the Hindus, because my mother was a devotee of Shri Krishna. She used to talk to me about Shri Krishna, and hence I created an image in my mind of Shri Krishna, with the flute, with all the devotion, all the love, all the songs, all the delight — you have no idea what a tremendous thing that is for the boys and girls of India. When I grew older and met with Bishop Leadbeater and the Theosophical Society, I began to see the Master K. H.—again in the form which was put before me, the reality from their point of view — and hence the Master K. H. was to me the end. Later on, as I grew, I began to see the Lord Maitreya. That was two years ago, and I saw Him then constantly in the form put before me.

I am telling you all this, not to obtain authority nor to create belief, but only in order to strengthen your own beliefs, your own hopes, your own minds and your own hearts. It has been a struggle all the time to find the Truth, because I was not satisfied by the authority of another, or the imposition of another, or the enticement of another. I wanted to discover for myself, and naturally I had to go through sufferings to find out. Now lately, it has been the Buddha whom I have been seeing, and it has been my delight and my glory to be with Him.

I have been asked what I mean by "the Beloved". I will give a meaning, an explanation, which you will interpret as you please. To me it is all — it is Shri Krishna, it is the Master K. H., it is the Lord Maitreya, it is the Buddha, and yet it is beyond all these forms.

WHO BRINGS THE TRUTH

What does it matter what name you give? You are fighting over the World-Teacher as a name. The world does not know about the World-Teacher; some of us know individually; some of us believe on authority; others have experience of their own, and knowledge of their own. But this is an individual thing and not a question about which the world will worry. What you are troubling about is whether there is such a person as the World-Teacher who has manifested Himself in the body of a certain person, Krishnamurti; but in the world nobody will trouble about this question. So you will see my point of view when I speak of my Beloved. It is an unfortunate thing that I have to explain, but I must. I want it to be as vague as possible, and I hope I have made it so. My Beloved is the open skies, the flower, every human being.

I said to myself: until I become one with all the Teachers, whether They are the same is not of great importance; whether Shri Krishna, Christ, the Lord Maitreya, are one is again a matter of no great consequence. I said to myself: as long as I see Them outside as in a picture, an objective thing, I am separate, I am away from the centre; but when I have the capacity, when I have the strength, when I have the determination, when I am purified and ennobled, then that barrier, that separation, will disappear. I was not satisfied till that barrier was broken down, till that separateness was destroyed. Till I was able to say with certainty, without any undue excitement, or exaggeration in order to convince others, that I was one with my Beloved, I never spoke. I talked of vague generalities which everybody wanted. I never said: I am the World-Teacher; but now that I feel I am one with the Beloved, I say it, not

WHO BRINGS THE TRUTH

in order to impress my authority on you, nor to convince you of my greatness, nor of the greatness of the World-Teacher, nor even of the beauty of life, the simplicity of life, but merely to awaken the desire in your own hearts and in your own minds to seek out the Truth. If I say, and I will say, that I am one with the Beloved, it is because I feel and know it. I have found what I longed for, I have become united, so that henceforth there will be no separation, because my thoughts, my desires, my longings — those of the individual self — have been destroyed.

Hence I am able to say that I am one with the Beloved — whether you interpret it as the Buddha, the Lord Maitreya, Shri Krishna, the Christ, or any other name.

For sixteen years you have worshipped the picture which has not spoken, which you have interpreted as you pleased, which has inspired you, given you tranquillity, given you inspiration in moments of depression. You were able to hold to that picture because that picture did not speak, it was not alive, there was nothing to be kept alive; but now that the picture, which you have worshipped, which you have created for yourselves, which has inspired you, becomes alive and speaks, you say: Can that picture, which I worshipped, be right? Can it speak? Has it any authority? Has it the power to represent the World-Teacher? Has it the magnitude of His wisdom, the greatness of His compassion, fully developed and can it be manifest in one individual? These of course are questions which you must solve for yourselves. You remember the well-known story by Dostoievsky in which the Christ reappears? He had been preaching and He went at last to Rome, and the Pope invited Him, and in secrecy fell on his knees and

WHO BRINGS THE TRUTH

worshipped and adored Him, but kept Him imprisoned. He said: "We worship you in secrecy; we admit that you are the Christ; but if you go outside, you will cause so much trouble; you will create doubts, when we have tried to quell them."

Now that picture is beginning to get alive, and you cannot have anything real, you cannot have anything true, which is not alive. You may worship a tree in the winter-time, but it is much more beautiful in the spring, when the buds, when the bees and the birds, when all the worlds, begin to be alive. Through the years of winter you have been silent and not questioning yourselves very sincerely, it has been comparatively easy; but now you must decide for yourselves what it all means.

Before, it was easy to say that you expected a World-Teacher and it meant very little; but now you are face to face with the problem of that picture coming to life. Whether you are going to worship continually a mere picture, or worship the reality of that picture, must, of course, be left to the individual. But do not, please, try to use your authority to persuade another, as I do not use mine to convince you of the truth of that picture being alive. To me it is alive. Though I used to worship that picture, I was not satisfied in the mere worshipping. I wanted to find out, to get behind the frame of that picture, to look through the eyes, think through the mind, feel through the heart of that picture. I was not satisfied, and because of my dissatisfaction, because of my discontentment, because of my sorrows, I was able to identify myself with the picture and hence I am the picture.

There is nothing very complicated about it, nothing

WHO BRINGS THE TRUTH

very mysterious, nothing to be excited about in order to convince others. It is when you are willing to put yourself under some authority that you will be broken — and quite rightly — because authority varies from day to day. One day it will be one person, another day it will be another, and woe to the man that bends to any or all of them. That is the very thing that you must not have, and that is what you are trying to bring about. You want an authority that will give you courage, that will make you develop more fully; but no external authority will ever give you the power to develop. Whether the truth which the picture speaks, when it has come to life, is of importance or not must be examined by yourselves.

It has been my practice to listen to everybody, always. I desired to learn, from the gardener, from the pariah, from the untouchable, from my neighbour, from my friend, from everything that could teach, in order to become one with the Beloved. When I had listened to all, and gathered the Truth wherever I found it, I was able to develop myself fully. Now, you are waiting for the Truth to come out of one person. You are waiting for that Truth to be developed, to be forced upon you by authority, and you are worshipping that person instead of the Truth.

When Krishnamurti dies, which is inevitable, you will make a religion, you will set about forming rules in your minds, because the individual, Krishnamurti, has represented to you the Truth. So you will build a temple, you will then begin to have ceremonies, to invent phrases, dogmas, systems of beliefs, creeds, and to create philosophies. If you build great foundations upon me, the individual, you will be caught in that house, in

WHO BRINGS THE TRUTH

that temple, and so you will have to have another Teacher come and extricate you from that temple, pull you out of that narrowness in order to liberate you. But the human mind is such that you will build another temple round Him, and so it will go on and on.

But those who understand, who do not depend on authority, who hold all peoples in their hearts, will not build temples — they will really understand. It is because a few have truly desired to help other people, that they have found it simple. Others who have not understood, although they talk a great deal about it, and of how they will interpret the teaching, will have difficulties. It is perfectly simple for me to go out into the world and teach. The people of the world are not concerned with whether it is a manifestation, or an indwelling, or a visitation into the tabernacle prepared for many years, or Krishnamurti himself. What they are going to say is: I am suffering. I have my passing pleasures and changing sorrows — have you anything lasting to give? You say you have found Happiness and Liberation — can you give me of that, so that I can enter into your kingdom, into your world? That is all they are concerned about and not the badges, the orders, the regulations, the books.

They want to see the living waters that flow under the bridge of human beings, so that they can swim with those waters into the vast ocean. And what you are concerned with all the time is how you are going to interpret. You have not found the Truth for yourselves, you are limited, and yet you are trying to set other people free. How are you going to do it? How are you going to discover what is true, what is false, what is the World-Teacher, what is reality, if you have

WHO BRINGS THE TRUTH

not cleared the stagnation from the pool so that it will reflect the Truth?

I have always in this life, and perhaps in past lives, desired one thing: to escape, to be beyond sorrow, beyond limitations, to discover my Guru, my Beloved — which is your Guru and your Beloved, the Guru, the Beloved who exists in everybody, who exists under every common stone, in every blade of grass that is trodden upon. It has been my desire, my longing, to become united with Him so that I should no longer feel that I was separate, no longer be a different entity with a separate self. When I was able to destroy that self utterly, I was able to unite myself with my Beloved. Hence, because I have found my Beloved, my Truth, I want to give it to you.

I am as the flower that gives scent to the morning air. It does not concern itself with who is passing by. It gives its scent, and those who are happy, who are suffering, will breathe that scent. But those who are contented, who are not longing, who do not care, who have no idea of the delights of the scent, will pass by unheeding. Are you going to compel them to stop and breathe that scent? You are concerned with how you are going to convince them. Why should you convince them? You will only convince those who are really searching. It is because you are doubting in your own search, that you are not searching truly. You are satisfied with your little knowledge, your little authorities. You want those authorities to speak, to save you from your doubts.

Suppose a certain person was able to tell you that I am the World-Teacher, in what way would it help, in what way would it alter the Truth? In what way would

WHO BRINGS THE TRUTH

understanding come to your heart, and knowledge come to your mind? If you depend on authority, you will be building your foundations on the sands, and the wave of sorrow will come and wash them away. But if you build your foundations in stone, the stone of your own experience, of your own knowledge, of your own sorrows and your own sufferings, if you are able to build your house on that, brick by brick, experience upon experience, then you will be able to convince others.

Until now you have been depending on the two Protectors of the Order for authority, on someone else to tell you the Truth, whereas the Truth lies within you. In your own hearts, in your own experience, you will find the Truth, and that is the only thing of value. That alone will satisfy your afflictions, that alone will clear away your sorrows, and that is why I feel I have got to speak of these things.

I could not have said last year, as I can say now, that I am the Teacher; for had I said it then it would have been insincere, it would have been untrue. Because I had not then united the Source and the Goal, I was not able to say that I was the Teacher. But now I can say it. I have become one with the Beloved. I have been made simple. I have become glorified because of Him, and because of Him I can help. My purpose is not to create discussions on authority, on manifestations in the personality of Krishnamurti, but to give the waters that shall wash away your sorrows, your petty tyrannies, your limitations, so that you will be free, so that you will eventually join that ocean where there is no limitation, where there is the Beloved.

I hope I have made it clear. To the minds that will understand, it should be clear. The minds and the

WHO BRINGS THE TRUTH

hearts that have groped, that have searched, that have longed to find the Truth — they will find it. You are not going to convince, to alter the mode of life in those who do not desire to alter. But as I have changed and become one with the Beloved, as I have found my end, which is the end for all, and as I have become united with the end, because I have affection — and without affection you cannot attain the end — because I bear love, because I have suffered and seen and found all, naturally it is my duty, it is my pleasure, my dharma, to give it to those who have not.

Whether I give it through the Order of the Star, or through any other body, that is of no value. People are not going to be concerned through what body it comes. They are only going to be satisfied if their sorrows, their pleasures, their passing vanities, their fleeting desires, can be killed and a greater thing than these established.

When once you understand the Truth of this Liberation and of this Happiness, it will set you free from yourselves, from all your vanities, pleasures, afflictions and sorrows. As I have attained Liberation, I want to give of it. But you say: You must give it in a certain fashion, you must be able to give it in a certain phraseology, in a certain fashion of language. Does it really matter out of what glass you drink the water, so long as that water is able to quench your thirst? Does it really matter who feeds you, so long as by that food you are satisfied and strengthened?

Because you have been accustomed for centuries to labels, you want life to be labelled. You want Krishnamurti to be labelled, and in a definite manner, so that you can say: Now I can understand — and then you think there will be peace within you. I am afraid it is not

WHO BRINGS THE TRUTH

going to be that way. Can you bind the waters of the sea? People have tried, but there is always disaster. I do not want to be bound, because that means limitation. You cannot bind the air. You can hold it, you can pollute it, you can put poison in that air, but the air which is outside, which is for all, you can never control. I am not going to be bound by anyone. I am going on my way, because that is the only way. I have found what I wanted. I have been united with my Beloved, and my Beloved and I will wander together the face of the earth.

You will never be able to force people, whatever authority, whatever dread, whatever threats of damnation you may use. That age is past. This is an age of revolution and of turmoil. There is a desire to know everything for oneself, and because you have not that desire inside you, you are being kept in the world of limitation. You think you have found, but you have not found. Because you have been made certain in your little uncertainties, you think you can convert the world.

When the Eiffel Tower was built, it thought itself the most beautiful, the most wonderful, the highest thing in the world, till a small aeroplane came flying over it. You are all thinking that you can run with the deer and roar with the lion, but you can only run with the deer and roar with the lion when you have become united with the Beloved. It is no good asking me who is the Beloved. Of what use is explanation? For you will not understand the Beloved, until you are able to see Him in every animal, in every blade of grass, in every person that is suffering, in every individual.

So, friend, the only thing that matters is that you should give the waters that will quench the thirst of the

WHO BRINGS THE TRUTH

people — the people who are not here, who are in the world. And the water that will give satisfaction, that will purify their hearts, ennoble their minds, is this: the finding of the Truth, and the establishing in their own minds and in their own hearts of Liberation and Happiness.

BY WHAT AUTHORITY
OMMEN CAMP FIRE TALKS 1927

BY WHAT AUTHORITY

I

During my talks here every evening I want to point out the way and to arouse in you the necessary strength so that you will be able to discover for yourselves your own source of greatness, your own source of nobility, the beginning of your own aspiration and of the desire to achieve Liberation and Happiness. In doing that and in giving you an explanation of what I mean by Liberation and Happiness, I must ask you to set aside, all the time, your own conceptions and enter into my thoughts and feelings, so that you will be able to understand from my point of view what is meant by Liberation and by Happiness. In order to facilitate your thought, so that you will be able to dig deep within yourselves, I am going to tell you a story.

Once upon a time, there was a flame of immense magnitude, of great height, reaching to the heavens, and out of that flame came many sparks and among those many sparks there was created, from one spark, a human being, and that human being we shall call, for the moment, Krishnamurti. I take that story because I know Krishnamurti well and as I shall examine him impersonally, I am going to ask you to do the same. Before I begin with my story, I want you to detach yourselves from your individualities, so that you will be able to examine yourselves as I am going to examine Krishnamurti.

That spark, through æons of time, through endless passage of time, became a human being. At first that human being was in the shape of a savage. He had, like all savages and barbarians, one desire, and that was the satisfaction of the physical; he gave way to the desires of the body, the pleasures of the body; to him the existence of life, the purpose of life, the end of life, was in the mere satisfaction of those desires and those cravings that are of the body. During many lives he learned, he suffered, he learned to acquire, he learned to possess, he learned to gather everything for himself. He was not happy till he had many possessions, many acquisitions — all things that perish. He dwelt in the winter time of ignorance; while he was young in evolution, he had only one purpose and that was the mere satisfaction of the body and the pleasures of the body. But through the passage of time, through sorrow, he began to learn the laws of the community, the laws that exist for the benefit of all, and through observing those laws and obeying those laws, he began to distinguish what is true and what is lasting from what is false and what is fleeting. He began, by the breaking of those laws, to suffer; and through many lives he was acquiring experience, till he grew to the state of a civilised being. Through many æons, through the passage of time, through years of suffering, and longing to escape from those things which the world considers are essential for the well-being and the Happiness of human beings, he sought for knowledge. Because, he said to himself, wherever I go, wherever I live, there is misery, there is turmoil around me and within me, and in order to escape this turmoil, in order to escape this limitation, this unhappiness, I must go out, seek and wander, to discover that which is lasting, that which is permanent.

He began to depend on other people for his Happiness, he began to depend on others for his affection, on others for his love, on others for his worship; in this search for

BY WHAT AUTHORITY

the lasting truth, he began to lose himself in temples, in ceremonies, at the altars, in all those things which are limiting and binding, but he was not satisfied and he was in constant revolt. He desired to extricate himself from those shrines that are by the wayside leading to the mountain-top. His desire was intense to discover what lay behind the picture which he was worshipping, what was behind the eyes and the mind of that image which was put before him, which he had worshipped life after life. To discover what lay behind the eyes, behind the heart of that picture, he went through immense sorrows, great disappointments and intense longings. Little by little, by austerities, by tortures, by starvation, in many lives, he was able to control his body, and while he was controlling his body, he was training at the same time his emotions and his mind; because when they are not cooperating, when they are not coordinated, when they are not synthetic, then there is discord, then there is no well-being.

As the fisherman goes out to sea on the open waters to gather fish, so he started on life to gather experience and while gathering experience he was caught in his own net and he had to cut himself loose from that net of experience to be free, to enter into that flame which is the essence of all experience. Little by little that person whom you know as Krishnamurti, who started as a separate spark, as a separate being from the flame, has been able, through great experiences, to be united with the flame.

I have told you that story, because ordinarily, when an individual starts as a separate being, it takes æons, it takes centuries of time to acquire all the lessons, all the teachings that life can give before there is the possi-

BY WHAT AUTHORITY

bility of perceiving, of seeing that vision of Liberation and Happiness. But for everyone of you who is here, it is possible now to perceive that vision of Liberation and Happiness, because you are now in the presence of the Beloved, and when the Beloved is with you, time as such ceases. You need not go through all the experiences of sorrow, of affliction, of grief, of intense joy, to perceive that goal which is the end for all. As the river at the beginning of its course knows its end and seeks sedulously to enter that sea, so you must know from the very beginning of your days, the end which awaits all.

I am saying this, not to impose authority, not to make you credulous, not to make you give devotion to the personality of one being. I am telling you all this because when you have become united with the Beloved, when you have merged into the flame, you can then go out and give that Happiness and that Liberation to others; you can give to those who are hungry, the Happiness that is lasting; you can give to those who are held in a prison of sorrow and grief, the vision of Liberation. You can but give it, you can but show it, but the individual must struggle to attain it. For authority can be cut down as the tree; and if you have not roots deep within you, well established in the ground, your tree will die, and will have to be re-planted. But if you have the roots well and firmly established, then it will sprout and bear tender leaves and buds and give shelter once more. And in telling you of this attainment of Liberation and Happiness, I am going to urge every one of you to think not of the individual that is speaking, but to go within and examine yourselves. Because I have found my Happiness, because I have found my tranquillity and my peace, because I have been united with my

BY WHAT AUTHORITY

Beloved, I would have you do the same. And to do that, to feel that union with the Beloved, there must be within you the strong and pure heart, the clear and tranquil mind. As the sun shines on all, on the daisy and on the forest tree, and helps them to grow, so, when the Beloved is with you, you will grow to your fullest measure, no matter at what stage of evolution you may be.

For such is the purpose of life: to start as the spark of a flame, to gather experience, and eventually to re-join the flame, so that the individual self is destroyed. Happy is he who has been able to unite himself with the Beloved. Happy is he, for he will be able to help others, for he will be able to give of the living waters of life to those that are thirsty, to those that are in want.

So, friend, I want you to realise from the very beginning that Happiness does not depend on any other individual, but on yourself. It has been my intense longing to unite with my Beloved, and it has been fulfilled because it has been my purpose from the very ancient of days. Now, while the Beloved is with you, when there is the possibility of seeing that vision, of holding that vision and well establishing it within your heart and within your mind, I want you to set aside and destroy all things that separate you and so become one with the Beloved. There is a great opportunity, there is a great possibility of attainment for you, if you feel strongly and intensely enough.

It is my purpose to show you that within you lies the strength and the power to attain and to establish within yourself Happiness and Liberation, so that when you go out into the world, you will be able to speak with your own authority which is born out of your own experience.

BY WHAT AUTHORITY

II

This afternoon I was walking in the garden where the flowers were in full bloom. There was a border of varied flowers and every flower had reached the culmination, the fruition of its being, had fulfilled its function and blossomed into the world giving pleasure to man. It had waited the whole summer to blossom out and bring forth its scent and give of that scent to the man who delights in beauty.

In the same way man is searching everywhere for the fulfillment of himself, in all climes, in all places, under all skies. Through political, social and economic activity, he is seeking for the fruition, for the development of himself through Happiness. All people of the world, whether they be in the East or in the West, whether their skin is yellow, brown, black, or white, they are all seeking Happiness. Happiness is the heritage of all, Happiness is the goal for all, Happiness is the end for all — the Happiness that outlasts all touch of sorrow, that is eternal, that is permanent, that is the fruition of the accumulation of all experience. There is such a permanent, lasting, indestructible Happiness, but man must seek for it through the passing stages of unhappiness. Go where you will, there you will find man seeking Happiness in perishable things. Whether it be in the East or in the West, all suffer alike, all have the same sorrows, the same afflictions, the same desires, the same agonies; and all are seeking for that Happiness, which dwells ever within, which is eternal. Man seeks in trivial things for that Happiness which is everlasting, for that Happiness which is Liberation. If he be hungry, he seeks to satisfy his stomach; if he be sorrow-laden,

BY WHAT AUTHORITY

his Happiness lies in forgetting himself. The Sannyasi, the man who has renounced the world and withdrawn into the secluded valley, seeks that Happiness; the creator, the artist, the genius seeks for that Happiness which will last, which will stand the test of time, which will give him strength, which will give him vitality to withstand the onslaughts of sorrow, of grief and of affliction. But in search of that Happiness which is lasting, they lose themselves in the impermanent. Of what use is the Happiness that can be destroyed? Of what use is it to be momentarily delighted when that delight disappears? Of what use is creation which gives momentary pleasure when that which you have created is destroyed?

Wherever you go, wherever you wander, there is a longing search to discover an abode where you can dwell peacefully and in tranquillity, where you can become one with that Kingdom of Happiness. There are many ways of seeking and attaining that Happiness, but the end, the goal, is the same for all, to whatever temperament or type a man may belong. Whatever his mode of activity in the world may be, the goal for him is the attainment of Happiness and Liberation. For when once you have perceived that end, to attain it you will throw aside all transient things, all those things which pass away with the touch of sorrow.

You will find that the man — under whatever clime — who is seeking for that Kingdom, which he knows dwells within, is like the butterfly, wandering from one flower to another, gathering honey. He is always looking outwards, always trying to find that Happiness, that beauty, that comfort, that Liberation in the outward manifestation. And while he is wandering outward in the world

BY WHAT AUTHORITY

of shadow, he is caught as in a net in the world of the unreal, and hence he begins to create karma. What he sows he will reap; whatever his actions may be, they will bear their own fruit. He cannot escape, and so he is caught continually in that world of transient things: from one sorrow he goes to another sorrow, from great sorrows to greater sorrows, from little pleasures to greater pleasures. While sorrow and fleeting pleasure cage him and hold him, he cannot go into that Kingdom where lies eternal Happiness.

That Kingdom of Happiness lies not in the world of manifestation, where there are shadows and decay, but within each one of you, and it is there that you must turn and seek. As the flower contains the scent, as the flower hides divinity within itself, so within each one of you lies the Kingdom of Happiness, whatever be your stage of evolution, whatever be your griefs or afflictions. When once you have discovered it within yourselves, then you can wander forth from the real to the unreal.

I want, for the moment, to give you an image so as to make it clear to you that the goal for all human beings is Liberation and Happiness. Let us imagine for a moment the top of a mountain where there are the last rays of a setting sun, where the beauty of the past day is concentrated. On that mountain are various stages, various sheltering huts, and each shelter invites you to stop and worship the particular god that it holds. And so man, though he knows that there is an ultimate goal, stays in these huts, enjoying himself and wasting his time, hence creating unnecessary karma which binds him to the wheel of life and death. So he must pass through those stages, rest in every shelter, if he is weak and has not sufficient strength and sufficient will to climb to the

BY WHAT AUTHORITY

top. To acquire that will, that determination, that purposefulness, he must go within and awaken himself to the Reality which lies there.

Most of you worship a picture, and when that picture becomes alive you wish that it had not, for that picture will tell you to go within yourselves, and not to worship that which is destructible, a mere canvas that can be torn. When that picture tells you to go within and there discover the Kingdom of Reality, the Kingdom of Truth, the Kingdom of Happiness and Liberation, you find it difficult because it requires thought, it requires training, it requires self-examination, self-criticism, which very few of you are willing to go through. You require some great miracle to transport you to the mountain-top. You are waiting for some Divine Manifestation to exhibit Himself miraculously, amidst thunder and lightning, and give you some medicine which will transform you, purify you and give you strength to leap to the mountain-top.

But, friend, the Truth lies in you; and because I have found that Truth, because I have identified myself with that Truth, and because my Beloved and I are one in my heart, I would tell you how to open those gates which will let you into your own heart, into your own mind, where you will find peace and tranquillity. But you must know what is sorrow, what is suffering, what is affliction, what are pleasures that are imperishable, what are pleasures that are lasting. Wisdom comes out of experience, and understanding out of a pure heart; and if there is no experience, if the heart is not willing to understand, you will remain long in the shelters on the upward mountain path. And because you have the Beloved with you, you can leave all those shelters and become the Beloved.

BY WHAT AUTHORITY

There lies the greatness of the moment, for there be very few days of summer, days when you can gather in your hay, when you can prepare your house and put all things in order, to welcome the Guest; because you will find that the Beloved is yourself — ennobled, glorified, yourself made perfect. And when once you have found Him within your heart and well established Him in your mind, then you have entered into that Kingdom of Happiness which is everlasting, into that Liberation which has no limitations.

So those who would seek Happiness and Liberation must wander within, must search out and find their own Kingdom. And when they have found that abode they will discover that it is the Kingdom for all — for all are searching, all are suffering and sorrow-laden. And those who have drunk at that fountain, who have developed that wisdom which is the outcome of experience, can go out and give to the afflicted of that lasting Happiness which is Liberation.

III

I should like you to listen diligently this evening to the voice of my words and understand its full meaning, so that there may be comprehension both of the mind and of the heart. I desire this evening, if I can, to take you into my heart and into my mind and to show you how my dream has been realised, how I have found my tranquillity and my peace — that peace which gives Happiness and Liberation — and how it has been given to me to behold and to possess my Beloved. And that you may understand and comprehend fully, I would beg you not to use me as an authority, because it is my

BY WHAT AUTHORITY

purpose to lead you into your own hearts, if you would follow me, so that you will there meet with my Well-Beloved and there enter on the path of peace where there is certainty, where there is no shadow of doubt. That you may understand me fully, I must make you realise the Truth for the moment, and perhaps for the rest of your life, so that you will be able to shatter your prejudices, the walls that you have erected during this life around the conception and the understanding of the Truth. For I would that you should completely destroy your narrowness, your limitations, and the things that you have acquired, the things that have become part of your being, which have made you narrow, which have perverted the judgment of Truth. What I am going to say is very simple, so simple that the complicated mind cannot understand, because the complicated heart and the complicated mind seize and pervert the Truth. What I say must not be taken as an authority to convince others, or even to convince yourself.

I know that many in this Camp are troubled about certain subjects that need clearing, that need understanding, and it is my purpose this evening to tell you that it will be fatal if we fight over words. There are people in this Camp, and in the world, who demand that in order to believe, in order to understand something that is very simple — for great truth is always simple and direct — there must be a miracle. I was told by someone that before he could believe that I am that which I profess to be, there must be a miracle. What greater miracle can there be than that you should understand and grasp the Truth? What greater miracle need there be than that a person should be able to lead you into your own hearts, into your own minds, and there

BY WHAT AUTHORITY

help you to discover the Truth? What miracle need there be to understand the smooth waters that flow down to the sea and the boisterous, dancing waters of the sea itself, or to understand the pure, beautiful rose, or the clear skies and a solitary cloud? What conviction need there be on the part of the beholder, on the part of the seeker, on the part of the sufferer, to alter his course of thought, his attitude of mind? I know it is much more difficult to believe the Truth, to be convinced of the Truth than to be hypnotised by a miracle. If I were able to perform a miracle, you would at once believe. But conviction is not born through transient things; the miracle is for the moment, but the Truth is eternal and permanent. And because I would take you into my heart, and would give of that understanding which I possess, I ask you to set aside all your complications, all your theories, all your judgments, so that you can understand the Truth.

It has been given to me, as I said, to be able, as an individual, to attain a certain altitude where I perceive life differently from the ordinary human being, where life which possesses most people does not possess me, where life is understood in its simplicity and in its purity. It has been given to me to attain this Happiness and this Liberation. For it is in freeing, in liberating oneself from all narrowing affections, from all sorrows, afflictions and griefs, that one truly attains the eternal Happiness. It is my purpose to give of that understanding, of the waters of life which shall satisfy the thirsty, and I shall do it, whether people call me by one name or by another name. And it is because of that intense, burning desire to give, that I would take you to my heart and give you the understanding which I possess. The Truth

BY WHAT AUTHORITY

lies in giving Happiness to others, that lasting Happiness which will liberate them from their own afflictions, from their own pettiness, from their own narrowness, from their limitations and from their prejudices. And I shall be able to do it, because in me I possess that fountain. Do not let us quarrel, do not let us disagree over a word. What matters is that you should understand the Truth, because you are suffering, because you are longing to find the Truth which I have found, because you are caught in the wheel of life and death, and desire to escape from its limitation.

It does not matter who gives you the Truth, who gives you the understanding that will enable you to climb to the mountain-top where you will discover yourself and the Kingdom of Happiness. If you worship the personality, the personality of Krishnamurti, if you give your affection to that being, you will suffer, because that being passes away, is destroyed and decays, because it is a transient thing. While if you are the disciples of the Truth, then you will become part of that Truth. When you see the beauty of a sunset, that sunset does not give you a moral code, it does not give you laws, regulations, dogmas, creeds, but if you become part of that beauty, then you need never worry about laws, regulations, modes of life, moral laws and so on. If you have that understanding, you will not be held in the net of transient things, of complicated things that have no value.

In saying all this, I do not wish to exercise authority, but to convince you of your own value, of your own strength, to multiply your own desires so that you may achieve, so that you may give. Whether I am this or that, or whether I am that which I profess to be, is of

BY WHAT AUTHORITY

no value. That which I am, remains with me. That which I am not, falleth away from me. That which I have gained, that which I possess, that which is part of me, can never go.

So, with that understanding, let us examine the question. The world — what does it desire? It desires people who have found the Truth, who are not swamped by creeds, by dogmas, by quarrels. It does not care what you think of me, or what I think of you, but it desires to drink of that knowledge which you possess, and if you dissipate yourselves in these petty discriminations, you are oblivious of the needs of those people who are suffering, who are afflicted, those people who are longing to find the Truth.

As I have said, I am burning with the desire to give you such an understanding that you will rid yourselves of all your jargons, all your systems, all your philosophies, such an understanding as will put a mirror before you, so that you will see yourselves as you are, so that you will from that vision gather strength in order to climb. To discover yourself, to find yourself, to strengthen yourself, is all that matters, and not your dogmas, your creeds, your philosophies. Because you all suffer, you want to be mesmerised by words, you want to be hypnotised by soft-sounding, melodious notes, but you can never by these means destroy the cause of sorrow; you may pass it by for a season but it will return as inevitably as the sunrise. In order to destroy that sorrow, in order to annihilate that which creates sorrow, you must go within and discover the world of reality, the world of Liberation, the world of Happiness.

The world problem is the individual problem; if the individual is at peace, has Happiness, has great tolerance,

BY WHAT AUTHORITY

and an intense desire to help, then the world problem as such ceases to exist. You consider the world problem before you have considered your own problem. Before you have established peace and understanding in your own hearts and in your own minds, you desire to etablish peace and tranquillity in the minds of others, in your nations and in your states; whereas peace and understanding will only come when there is understanding, certainty and strength in yourselves.

What is the purpose of life? Why do you suffer? Why are you afflicted? Why have you to weep? Why have you to exercise control? Why have you to struggle? It is a process of evolution from the very beginning, from the very foundation of the earth, from the time when the spark starts forth on its individual progress. While it is climbing towards that mountain-top, it accumulates those things that are unnecessary, and through this accumulation it creates karma, and gradually, as it progresses on that upward path, it begins to discard, it becomes more simple, until it joins the flame and becomes the Truth itself. From the flame you came forth, to the flame you will return and thus unite the beginning and the end. The purpose of life is to lose the separate self which started as an individual spark and when you have done that, then the Truth is established within you and you become part of the Truth, and you are yourself the Truth.

When you go away from here, people will question you, and because they see the light in your face and Happiness in your heart, they will desire to share it. In what manner are you going to give it? Are you going to say: "You must believe in such-and-such an individual with such-and-such a label"? Or are you

BY WHAT AUTHORITY

going to say: "He has opened my heart and has given me understanding and I wish to share it with you"? By that alone you will be judged, and by that alone you will be able to help. People do not require names, labels, badges, societies and orders; they are not going to be satisfied by creeds and dogmas and enforced beliefs, but by understanding, sympathy and affection. They require that water which shall quench their thirst, which shall quench their burnings and their longings, and pacify and give them certainty, and hence strength, in themselves. If you make use of authority — it does not matter whose it is — you are limiting them to that particular authority, and they will suffer and the time will come when they will desire to free themselves from that authority.

That Truth which dwells in each one of you must be uncovered, and in me lies the power to give you encouragement, as the sun shines on the daisy as well as on the rose. If you have the longing, if you have sufficient understanding and purpose, you will understand the Truth in its pure sense, in its simplicity; but if you are complicated, you will pervert it. The river which meanders down to the sea feeds all the peoples of the world, without concerning itself as to whether they be brown, black, white or yellow. All that it remembers is that is must keep its source alive and undefiled, so that it may feed those people on its banks who are thirsty, and the trees that have roots deep under the earth. Whether man pollutes it by his machines or by his complications, is not its concern.

So, friends, because you have gathered from all parts of the world, and you will go away again and talk of all that you have heard here, I would that you could destroy

BY WHAT AUTHORITY

your misunderstandings of the Truth, your narrow judgments, your limitations, so that you will be able to give to those who are hungry, of that which will satisfy them eternally. And to do that, you have to set aside — as you put aside your cloak — your small theories, your complications, and become simple, as simple as a single star in a naked sky. When you see beauty, the beauty of the rose, the beauty of the sunset or of the sky, and you cannot appreciate and understand that beauty, it is of no use for me to tell you concerning the beauty of it. If you have a veil in front of your eyes, I may be able, perhaps, to tear it away, but if you have the power again to grow another veil, woe to you! When you go out, you must have understood the Truth, but if you have little understanding, little narrownesses, you will pervert the Truth, you will not be able to help others. I know you give your devotion, your love, to the personality of Krishnamurti, but that is not enough, friends. You must understand the Truth, you must, during these few days, go inside yourselves and there discover Krishnamurti, for there you will find him, as I have found my Beloved. And when you find him, you will have found peace, you will have entered on the path of peace, you will have opened the gates of Happiness and Liberation.

IV

In ancient days man retired from the turmoil and bustle of the world, and withdrew into the world of reality within himself to seek peace and Happiness. He secluded himself to search, to discover, to commune with himself and so to enter into that Kingdom where there

BY WHAT AUTHORITY

is Happiness, where there is Liberation. But as times are now, when you have to build both materially and spiritually, you must remain in the world and there find your Liberation and your Happiness. While building materially, you must at the same time build your spiritual strength, your spiritual determination, and be liberated from that very building itself. When the artist paints a picture, he is not attached to the picture, he is merely concerned with reproducing his ideas and materialising them on canvas; after he has done that, he is free. Likewise those of you who are still seeking, who are still groping, who would desire to enter into that realm of Happiness and of Truth which abides in each one, you must still live in the world of forms, the world of manifestation, the world of unreality, and there, working in the unreal you must discover the real. You must be of the Truth, part of the Truth, and yet work with the unreal and the fleeting. You cannot withdraw, as of yore, into forests, into monasteries, into quiet, secluded valleys to seek and to commune with yourself. That is not Liberation, that is mere self-attainment, that is mere self-seeking; those who would really attain in the times of to-day, while they are working in the world, while they are making the world beautiful and noble, and perfecting the transient things, even while they are struggling, while they are suffering and are afflicted, must seek that Liberation and that Happiness.

So if you look at it from that point of view, Liberation is not annihilation; on the contrary, it is construction; Liberation is not negative, but on the contrary, it is positive. It is not entering into a mere void and there losing yourself, but it is entering into Truth, becoming part of the Truth, and going out and liberating those

BY WHAT AUTHORITY

who are worshipping the reflections on the still pools; then you have great energies and vitality, then you are part of the world. When once you have attained Liberation and when once that Happiness becomes part of your being, then you realise that Liberation is constructive and not a mere vague dream. It is as tangible as that fire which you see, as alive and dancing as that flame. There are those who imagine that Liberation is the annihilation of the world, the entering into a void where there is no self. It is true that there is no separate self, but there is the Self of all; there the world is one; the flower, the blade of grass, the vast skies, every tree, every human being exists in that Kingdom. Because many have the idea that Liberation means the annihilation of all things around them, the destruction of the world of material welfare, of art, of science, of beauty, I would urge on you that it is rather in making those things that are around you more beautiful, more noble and more perfect, that you attain Liberation, although at the same time you must be detached from them all. As the scent of the flower is wafted through the air and leaves the flower as it was, so is the liberated man who gives freshness, who gives delight to every passerby. So those of you who would seek this Liberation and this Happiness must not only dream, must not only have contemplations and solitary retreats, but must work in the world of transient things, making the world beautiful, making it noble, and making human beings happy, even though these are temporary. In order to forget the physical, you must first perfect it; in order to attain, you must not neglect it.

For what profit is knowledge, understanding and wisdom, if you do not use that understanding, that wisdom

BY WHAT AUTHORITY

and that knowledge to break the fetters that bind you? Many of you are more learned in the ways of books than perhaps I am, many of you are much more aged in this life than I am, but because I have found my Liberation and because I have attained that Kingdom of Happiness which dwells within me, I would tell you that, if you would enter into that abode, you must be free from all fetters, you must destroy those cords of affliction which bind you. For wherever a soul is bound by affliction, by the cords of sorrow, he will be unable to enter within himself, he will be unable to see himself clearly. When he has renounced all things, then he will be able to control his mind and his heart, for the heart walketh after the eye and the mind followeth the heart. Unrest is constant until there is this intense desire to discover the Truth. Because you suffer from your own actions, from your own desires, from your own little knowledge, from your own little purposes, your own little deceits and little conceits, because you have not been able to rid yourselves of these, you will never be able to enter into that Kingdom which dwells within you.

There was a time when Krishnamurti, as an individual, desired to find Liberation, but, like all human beings, he was caught in the wheel of his own desires, of his own knowledge, of his own little conceits and deceits. Because he desired to reach that Truth which is the purpose of life, because he desired to destroy that separateness which existed between the Truth and his ignorance, he suffered, he was bound to the wheel of birth and death. But now he is consumed in the fire of Liberation and of Happiness, and exists no longer as a separate being because his desires, his creations, his self-expression, have become those of his Beloved.

BY WHAT AUTHORITY

Because it has been my purpose to show you that path of Liberation and Happiness and to open your heart so that you will enter into your own inward self and there discover the Truth, I would tell you that you must renounce all things. You must renounce your books — the books that bind you, the philosophies that restrict you, the works that encompass you. You must give up your friends to enter within yourself, you must give up your families. If you would go within and there discover the Truth as a single star in the sky, you must give up your gods, the rites they demand and the ceremonies they require. For if you seek to enter with all these burdens, you will be caught in their limitations, you will be caught in the shrines in which you worship, you will be held by superstitions, by dogmas and by creeds, and to escape from these very things you must renounce those things. I know it is easy and comforting to hide yourself behind books, behind philosophies, behind creeds and dogmas, behind gods and behind ceremonies, but as long as you are held by them, you will be limited, you will be bound and there will be fleeting joys and sorrows. The moment you leave these things behind — as a man passes through a bank of clouds — and enter within and there discover the Truth, you will become part of the Truth. Then you will need no supports, no crutches, but you will need strength, you will need determination and ecstasy of purpose. You must give up your narrowness, your pettiness, your little knowledge, in order to understand the simple truth. Because your mind is complicated, you will make the Truth complicated; because you have the knowledge of books and the authority of books, you will give to that Truth the authority and the knowledge of books.

BY WHAT AUTHORITY

So, friend, if you would learn to seek that Truth, if you would enter into that abode where lives the Truth like a flame that is ever dancing, that is ever enticing you, that is ever giving you energy to fulfil your purpose, you must set aside all things, you must give up all things and enter within. It is because it is so difficult to give up all things, because the Truth is so difficult to conquer that you need crutches. It is much easier to live in the secluded shrine than to live in solitude, in loneliness on the mountain-top. Though you may perceive the mountain-top in moments of tranquillity, in moments of peace, though you may occasionally enter within your heart and there discover the Truth for yourself, it requires great determination to cling to that Truth, for the world of unreality is much more real to those who have not entered into the Kingdom of Happiness, who have not tasted this freedom, and so you have to be supported by those things which have no value. But all things meet in the end; whether you come from one shelter or another, you will come to the same goal. And for those who have perceived the end, it becomes their purpose, their determination, and their duty to go forth and give life to those who have not yet seen, who have not yet felt, who have not yet the knowledge of such things.

V

We have another evening before this Camp is closed, and so I would desire that you should comprehend that which I have been explaining, before you leave. By now you must have all perceived in what way the Truth comes, where it lies and in what manner you must proceed in order to find it. In the discovering of that Truth

BY WHAT AUTHORITY

you pray, naturally, for comfort, but you should pray rather for understanding. For comfort passes, and understanding remains, as understanding is the residue of experience, as it is the wisdom that comes from maturity, from ripeness, from thought, from joys and sorrows. Comfort is pleasant, comfort is delectable, comfort is satisfying, but comfort does not give substance, does not enrich the soul — it merely stagnates, and forms a green scum over the mind.

I have found my Liberation and my Happiness through sorrow, through suffering and experience, through setting aside all things, through renouncing the gods I have worshipped; and because of that finding I would give.

Truth is generally not understood. Those who would gaze upon the sun need strong eyes, and there be very few who have such strong eyes. They need coloured glasses. And because Truth is dazzling, because Truth is powerful, annihilating and yet constructive, you do not desire Truth in all its nakedness, in all its purity; so you clothe it, you call it by pretty-sounding names, so as to comfort yourselves in those names. I know, as I have myself done it; it has been my lot to deceive myself behind coloured glasses so as not to be dazzled; but I had to remove those coloured glasses through sorrow, through suffering, through the desire and the incessant prayer for understanding. Before you can find the Truth, you require a clear understanding, and with it Truth will come. I have found the Truth which abides in everyone and which abides in me; I have found that Happiness which exists in all and in myself; I have found that Liberation which is in all and in myself; and if I am to give that Truth to you, you must remove those glasses that you have coloured with prejudice, through

BY WHAT AUTHORITY

little understanding, through little sorrows, through little pleasures.

You desire comfort, you desire substance, you desire knowledge and wisdom, but, friend, that knowledge, that substance, that wisdom come only when you can behold the Truth in its entire nakedness, when you can be one with the Truth and abide with that Truth. But those who would understand this Truth, this Truth of Happiness and Liberation, must set aside those things which they have accumulated, those things which have grown up and have hidden the Truth during the past. I would that you could find the Truth for yourself, the Truth of your own understanding, of your own creation, which is the same as my understanding and my creation. For authority is like a cloud. It darkens and it does not clear, it hides the face of the mountain, and hence that which you worship is hidden; but you should have all things open, clear and precise in your understanding. Then you will discover the Truth.

There must not be in your mind the fear of missing something. Many people are afraid, naturally, that because of their misunderstanding or their lack of understanding of the Truth, they will not see the glory of the Beloved. But, friend, if you would see the glory, if you would see the face of the Beloved, you must have a pure heart and a tranquil mind. Then you will have the power to discriminate, the power to choose, the power to set aside those things which are trivial, those things which are transient.

And so I would ask you not to crave for comfort, but for understanding, for with understanding you have judgment, with understanding you have tolerance and affection; without these, woe to the man who searches

BY WHAT AUTHORITY

for Truth, for he will be bound by his own fetters. So I would ask you to have understanding and not a definite set of beliefs, of dogmas, of authorities, of credulities. Then you will be able to help, then you will be able to become the real disciples of the Beloved, then you will have the Beloved with you.

Like everyone else Krishnamurti, in the past, searched, obeyed and worshipped, but as time grew, as suffering came, he wanted to discover the reality which hides behind the picture, behind the sunset, behind the image, behind all philosophies, behind all religions, all sects, all organisations, and to discover and to understand that, he had to hang on to a peg of unreality, of untruth, till, little by little, he was able to pass all those shrines that are limiting, that are binding, all the gods that insist on worship. In passing all those he was able to arrive where all religions, where all affections are consummated, where all worship ends, where all desire ceases, where the separate self is purified by being destroyed. It is because I have gone through those stages that I am able to speak with the authority of my own experience, with the authority of my own knowledge, and I would give to you of that knowledge, of that experience.

The guide knows the short mountain-path, and though it be dangerous, though there be great obstacles to climb, though there be many pitfalls, if you would be as the guide himself, you must follow the guide who knows — follow not blindly, not superstitiously, not in credulity, but through your own desire to find the Truth, through your own suffering, through your own desire to set aside those things which are fetters, which are holding you as cords of affliction. So, if you would follow me into your own hearts, where there lies this Truth, where

BY WHAT AUTHORITY

dwells the Beloved, you must have a mind that is trained through understanding, that is unprejudiced, that is not bound, that is not limited in its vision of greatness. For prejudice hides and does not make clear, prejudice is like the cloud which hides the sun, and most people prefer to dwell behind the cloud rather than in front of it where there is no barrier between themselves and the clear sun. So if you have a mind that is without prejudice, that is not narrow, that is understanding, Truth will come, Truth will invite you into its abode, which is your own heart, which is your own understanding.

Then you must have a tranquil heart, a heart that is affectionate, yet detached and impersonal. It is essential to love, for through love you grow, you expand, you live as the bird lives in the free air, joyous at all times. So must be a heart which is full of affection, but it must be detached, impersonal and able to give its affection to all, and not to one individual alone, or to one particular group.

Then you must have a body made perfect with understanding; for without a clean, fine body, there is illhealth. So when you have the mind, the emotions and the body in perfect cooperation, assisting each other, developing each other, encouraging each other, that veil which separates you from the Truth will be destroyed. Then will come that which you desire, the comfort of understanding, not the comfort of stagnation. As on the pools in the woods where there have not been many winds, where the life has not been, where the birds do not alight, you will find a green scum, you will find that no animal comes to drink, that no human being delights there, you will find that there is no reflection of the heavens or of the open skies or of the flying birds,

BY WHAT AUTHORITY

so is the mind, so is the emotion, so is the body which is comforted. But the moment you desire to seek understanding, the moment you desire to have that Truth within you, then you are as the dancing waters of the sea; you will have your calmness, your moments of tranquillity, but you will also be like the rivers that dance down to the sea.

So those who follow the Truth, which abides in me, must discover their wisdom in their understanding, in their experience, in their sorrows, and in their joys. Of what avail is it to give a beautiful picture to a child? He would little understand its beauty. But give it to the real artist, give it to the man who has great understanding of pictures, and he will appreciate it, he will desire, not to copy, but to create it in himself, in his own fashion, in his own manner. Because you desire to copy, there is misery; because you desire authority, there is trouble; but if you desire to understand, if you desire to cooperate, if you desire to create in the light of that understanding, then you will not be troubled, then you will have found peace, then you will have established within you the delight of being ever with the Beloved. And, friend, in this short time that we have been together, some who have knowledge — not of mysterious things — will have found understanding; with them dwells the responsibility of cooperating with that understanding. When within you lies the glory of the Truth, you can develop it fully, as the flame develops when you throw logs of wood into it; or you can let that flame die down and wait for an æon, for centuries, to rekindle it so that it will give comfort, give warmth, give substance to the mind, to the heart that suffers.

BY WHAT AUTHORITY

VI

Once there was a mountain whose head was hidden beyond the clouds; around it there were vast plains, and valleys upon valleys. In search of that mountain-top, people gathered from all quarters of the world; people of many nationalities and of many types came there to discover the truth which the mountain held. Some came to examine the flora and the fauna of the mountain-side, others came to examine scientifically its strata, its height and its width, how much shadow it cast. People came to worship it, to rejoice in its glory, to see it and to carry back that memory to their homes and cherish it in their hearts. Some came to paint it, some came to photograph it, some came to take away little bits of earth and stone from the mountain, some came to perform ceremonies round about it, some came in order that they might tell of the truth of that mountain to others, some came and talked and heard their own echo — their laughter reached their own ears, back from the mountain.

Others came wanting knowledge, and desiring that the mountain should give them the solution for all their troubles. But its head was beyond the clouds, nearer the heavens, and there were very few who had climbed to the very top and who beheld from there the full view of all the peoples, all the temperaments, all the valleys and all the plains. So is Truth.

You who have gathered here from forty different countries, have come to worship the Truth, to discover the Truth, but you have come with your own understandings, with your own doubts, with your own encouragements, with your own wisdom, to discover, to understand, that which I have been holding up to you. You

BY WHAT AUTHORITY

have come to see me, the Truth, and you have come partly understanding, partly prejudiced, partly judging, partly perverting the Truth. He needs to be a strong man who would climb the mountain-top, who would understand the entire Truth in all its nakedness, in all its perfection. He needs to have a strong heart and a strong mind to contain it and to hold it, and strong eyes to see the vision, to see the glory of that Truth. People who come to worship an image, to worship the rocks of the mountain, only perceive a part of it and then return home convinced in their own little understandings, in their own little knowledge, in their own little wisdom. But unless you have the entire Truth, the absolute Truth in all its profundity, in all its simplicity, you are not the Truth. The part does not make the entire Truth; one aspect of the Truth does not give the full understanding of the whole Truth.

I have been desiring to give you the full Truth which abides within me, and which I have learned, through centuries, through many lives, to conquer and to establish well in my heart. You have come from different lands, with your different temperaments, with your different understandings, with your different wisdoms, and before you can accept this Truth fully, before you can understand it in all its nakedness, in all its simplicity, there must be purity of mind and tranquillity of heart. You all desire immediate solutions for your passing shadows of sufferings, passing shadows of afflictions, passing shadows of joys, and because the solution is never without, but is of your own understanding, of your own knowledge, of your own wisdom that abides within you, you are disappointed. Because you cannot understand the Truth in its entirety, there is puzzlement, there is confusion, there is questioning, there is doubt. You want all your sorrows, all your griefs, all your accumulations of ages to be swept aside by one brief momentary glimpse of the Truth. How can you keep the river clean, pure, undefiled, if the source is sullied? So you must return to the source and there begin anew, begin again to tread the very stages that you have already trodden; go over them in your minds, interpret them anew, so that you will grow straight as the fir tree on the mountain-top in solitude and in firmness. But this requires complete renunciation, your going through greater sorrows, greater pleasures and greater ecstasies, if you would arrive at that mountain-top which holds its head above the clouds of human understanding. So you have to begin where all people begin, for there only lies knowledge, there lies wisdom, there lies understanding which is in the mind and in the heart. If you have not a pure mind and a clean heart, if you have not a mind that has understanding and a heart that is sympathetic and affectionate, then whatever authority, whatever knowledge of books or of persons you may possess, it will all wither away as the leaf in the autumn.

So those who would climb to the heights of understanding and of Truth in all its fullness, in all its greatness and simplicity, must keep their minds and their hearts clean, strong and perfect. To do that you must watch, examine, criticise yourself and change constantly. You must needs be a strong man, you must needs be a man that is experienced in wisdom, before you can understand Truth in its fullness, in its greatness. If you would climb to those heights where lies the Truth, you must watch all your actions, you must watch all your thoughts, you must watch all your affections, for

BY WHAT AUTHORITY

they are limiting if they are not clean, if they are not pure, if they are not strong in proportion to the Truth. And who can help the weak man to climb to the mountain-top? He can only help himself, he can only gather strength to climb, from within himself. And so those who would desire the Truth that will destroy their sorrows, their fleeting affections, their passing desires and impermanent afflictions, must possess a strong, pure and clean heart. You must have wisdom, you must have experience, you must have the intuition that guides, and if you have not those, many suns will set, many years will pass, before you can perceive the Truth. And to acquire these, you must doubt, you must question every action, every thought that springs within you, and never be satisfied until you have gained that Truth which abides within you, till you are certain of your own Truth, till there is this certainty which is born out of great uncertainty — uncertainty of your purpose, uncertainty of your goal, uncertainty of your determination. Out of these uncertainties, immense, strong, purposeful certainty will be born.

Likewise beware of authority. Authority may comfort for a moment, but it is not the Truth, it is not lasting, it is not permanent; it is like the cloud across the fair sky, it passeth away and you are left naked, burning in the brilliant sun. So if you would have that knowledge which is your own, which is of your own creation, which is the outcome of your own experience, then you must go within, cleanse yourself of all those things which you have accumulated, cleanse yourself of those impurities; and, little by little, as the sun rises in the morning and disperses the mist by its warm rays, so in you there will be born the strength, the determination, the purpose to achieve the mountain-top. And there lies the only comfort, for what you gather from your own experience, from your own knowledge, is lasting, is permanent; and nobody, whoever he may be, can destroy that which you have created with your own hands, with your own sufferings, with your own afflictions. Out of that comes the desire to live nobly; for who can give the desire to live nobly except yourself? What heart, except his own, can prompt and urge a human being to tread the path of peace, the path of Liberation and of Happiness? Others may encourage, others may discourage, but in you alone lies the power to tread, in you alone lies the determination, in you alone lies the wisdom. If you would attain that Truth, if you would become perfect in the knowledge of that Truth, you must go through this process of renunciation, setting aside those things which have no value, putting aside your little knowledge in order to acquire greater knowledge, putting aside your little wisdom in order to acquire greater wisdom; and so when you reach the abode where there is no cloud of doubt, of misjudgment, where there is no question of perverting judgment, or of false thoughts, of false emotions, of fleeting affections, then you are truly in possession of the Truth, then truly are you like myself — the Beloved.

So those who have come from far-off lands to worship the mountain, will worship it, will photograph it, will carry away the earth and the stone which they have gathered, will examine the fairies, the angels, round about the mountain; but those who have climbed to the top will become the mountain, those who have reached the summit will know the delight of helping, of giving, of liberating others.

BY WHAT AUTHORITY

So, friends, you who have gathered from different nations to worship the mountain, should beware of what you take back; beware whether it be part of the Truth, or the full Truth. If it be a part, then let there be a burning desire within you to reach the very mountain-top, to become the Beloved, to become the Truth itself. And when you have reached that stage, as I have, when you have become the Beloved, as I have, then you will be able to give those waters of life that are eternal, then you will be able to satisfy the thirsty, then you will be able to give balm to the afflicted, then you will be the redeemers of the world. You are all walking by the light of the candle, but because I hold you in my heart, I would give you the light of the sun.

Now, this is our last evening, and you are all going away to different countries with part of the Truth; you are going away with greater burdens than you know of, you are going away to enrich your own lives and the lives of others. With a sun in your heart, with delight in your mind, you must create those things which are lasting, those things which will give eternal comfort to others. For one who has reached Liberation, for one who has achieved, for one who is in full possession of the Truth, there is no sorrow in parting. And because in me you all exist, for me there is no separation; but because you do not possess me, for you there is separation and sorrow. There is separation for those who, because of their little understanding of Truth, have not conquered the Truth, have not become part of the Truth. But if you bear that Truth in your heart, if you bear me, who am the end of all search, in your heart, then there will be no separation. In that strife, in that struggle to attain the mountain-top, there is unity both in affliction and in joy. So, friend, wherever you may go, if you have that Truth, you will not be lonely, you will not be depressed, you will need no comfort from without, you will need no truth except this one Truth.

THREE POEMS

THE SIMPLE UNION

THE GARDEN OF MY HEART

COME AWAY

THREE POEMS

THE SIMPLE UNION

Listen to me,
O friend.

Be thou a yogi, a monk, a priest,
A devout lover of God,
A pilgrim searching for Happiness,
Bathing in holy rivers,
Visiting sacred shrines,
The occasional worshipper of a day,
A great reader of books,
Or a builder of many temples —
My love aches for thee.
I know the way to the heart of the Beloved.

This vain struggle,
This long toil,
This ceaseless sorrow,
This changing pleasure,
This burning doubt,
This burden of life,
All these will cease, O friend —
My love aches for thee.
I know the way to the heart of the Beloved.

Have I pilgrimaged the earth,
Have I loved the reflections,
Have I chanted, singing in ecstasy,
Have I donned the robe,
Have I put on ashes,

THREE POEMS

Have I listened to the temple bells,
Have I grown old with study,
Have I searched,
Was I lost?
Yea, much have I known —
My love aches for thee.
I know the way to the heart of the Beloved.

O friend,
Wouldst thou love the reflection,
If I can give thee the reality?
Throw away thy bells, thine incense,
Thy fears and thy gods,
Set aside thy systems, thy philosophies.
Come,
Put aside all these.
I know the way to the heart of the Beloved.

O friend,
The simple union is the best.

This is the way to the heart of the Beloved.

THE GARDEN OF MY HEART

I am the path
Leading to the sheltered garden
Of thy heart,
O world.
I am the fountain
That feeds thy garden,

THREE POEMS

O world,
With the tears
Of my experience.

I am the scented flower
That beautifies thy garden,
The honey thereof,
The delight of thy heart.

Destroy thy weeds
In thy garden,
O world,
And keep thy heart
Pure and strong,
For there alone
I can grow.

Create no barriers
In the garden of thy heart,
O world,
For in limitation
I wither and die.

I have a garden
In my heart,
O world,
Where every flower
Speaketh of thee.

Open the gates
Of the garden of thy heart,
O world,
And let me in.

THREE POEMS

Without me
There shall be no shade,
Nor the soft breeze
From the cool mountains.

I have a garden in my heart,
O world,
That hath no beginning
And no end,
Where the mighty
Do sit with the poor,
Where the Gods
Do delight with the human.

Open as the vast skies,
Clear as the mountain stream,
Strong as the tree in the wind,
Is my heart.

Come,
O world,
Gather thy flowers
In the garden of my heart.

COME AWAY

As many scores of rivers
Enter into the sea,
So the understanding of the world
Has come unto me.
An immense longing
Is born unto me.
An aching love
Is burning my heart,

THREE POEMS

A passionate desire
Is consuming my being.

Come away,
Come away,
O world,
From thy changing sorrows,
From thy dying love.
I have found the way.

Come away,
Come away,
O world,
From thy little gods,
From the interpreters thereof.
I have found the way.

Come away,
Come away,
O world,
From thy fleeting passions,
From thy decaying achievements.
I have found the way.

Come away,
Come away,
O world,
From thy prison of pain,
From the keepers thereof.
I have found the way.

Come away,
Come away,

THREE POEMS

O world,
From thy burning desires,
From the agonies thereof.
I have found the way.

Come away,
Come away,
O world,
From the false,
From the burdens thereof.
I have found the way.

Come away,
Come away,
O world,
From thy kneeling,
From the holding of thy sad hands.
The temple walls be falling.
I have found the way.

Come away,
Come away,
O world,
For all things perish,
Though thy soft tears
Wash away thy memories.
I have found the way.

Seized am I
With a burning passion
To free thee
From thy cage,
For I have found the way.

THREE POEMS

The bird is on the wing,
And his voice fills my heart.
The vast firmament,
The limitless space
Enfold me.

I am thy Lover,
I am thy Teacher,
Renounce all
And follow me,
For my way
Is the way of Liberation.

Come,
Come away,
O love,
Sit beside me,
I will teach thee
The way to Happiness.

ORDER OF THE STAR
J. KRISHNAMURTI
HEAD OF THE ORDER

OBJECTS

1. TO DRAW TOGETHER ALL THOSE WHO BELIEVE IN THE PRESENCE OF THE WORLD-TEACHER IN THE WORLD.
2. TO WORK WITH HIM FOR THE ESTABLISHMENT OF HIS IDEALS.

Membership in the Order is open to all who subscribe to its objects. There are no fees for membership in the Order. Certain National Sections have found it convenient to fix a regular subscription, but this practice is not in any way binding on the Order as a whole.

There is a Chief Organizer for all International work. The Headquarters of the Order is established at Eerde, Ommen, Holland. The Order exists now in forty-five countries with a National Organizer in each country.

The badge of the Order is a five-pointed silver star. The Order publishes its magazine, THE STAR, in several countries simultaneously. An INTERNATIONAL STAR BULLETIN is also issued from the Headquarters at Eerde, Ommen, Holland.

AFTERWORD

By Paul Tice

The Order of the Star, as seen on the adjoining page, was the organization that supported Krishnamurti during the time he presented the talks that appear in this book. Its full name was The Order of the Star in the East. It was created by Annie Besant and the Theosophical society as a vehicle for ushering in a new world teacher, or Maitreya. Krishnamurti was specially chosen to fulfill that role, and was trained to do so from a young age.

The lectures given here, upon looking back, represent a major awakening in Krishnamurti's life. He did not hesitate to share it with his listeners. This important work was one of the last, if not the very last, to be published that represented his teachings while still head of the Order. It first appeared in 1928. Shortly thereafter, in 1929, Krishnamurti renounced his role in front of thousands of followers, dissolved the Order and returned all existing assets that had been bestowed upon him, including various properties and money.

His actions, without question, can be seen to have germinated from many of the ideas presented in this book. For him to have remained in his role as a world-wide prophesied messiah, or world teacher, would have been purely hypocritical based on this book, should he have chosen to stay. He encouraged others to seek the core of Truth within themselves, and not to depend on authority of any kind to tell you what that is. The Truth can only be found and experienced by each individual – only then does it become real enough, and powerful enough, to be genuinely recognized. With this book, the reader can see that Krishnamurti had committed himself to the coming separation. Those highest in the Order, even if awed by the wisdom this book contained, had to be equally frightened by it as well.

Once the separation occurred, many of Krishnamurti's 45,000 followers were confused and felt abandoned since they had believed he was the One they were waiting for. Krishnamurti's explanation caused them to search deeply – and many found freedom and their own Truth as a result. By renouncing the Order, Krishnamurti had, in fact, set many people free and helped to awaken them. This renunciation accomplished what his followers were *really* seeking from him – but had originally failed to get. It happened without the very object of their "worship."

It is this writer's opinion that Krishnamurti's role as a true world teacher began – really began – at the time that he had *renounced* it. In doing this, he also became totally free. One cannot teach freedom well without actually *being* free. From this time forward he never affiliated himself with any organization, teacher, dogmatic belief system, or set of teachings of any kind. He kept people looking for the truth with their own pure awareness. And he was a master at teaching this. Reading his work puts one's mind into an entirely new place – a place that often does not require the normal thinking process to understand. But it worked. People can get wrapped up too much in the continuous loop of thinking and processing information. When one can step back from it and quiet the mind, this other, pure awareness can often reveal itself. He knew how the human mind worked, taught us how to pry lose its treasures (or put it aside to find them), and is now considered one of the greatest spiritual teachers to have ever lived.

Whether you worshipped the God of a particular religion or followed Krishnamurti, it did not matter to him. In doing so, one is apt to believe that they are "right" and others who fail to follow this path are "wrong." He did not want to put himself into the position of making people wrong, and being "the answer," because he knew he was not. He refused to have followers. He wanted listeners, not followers. If people listened well enough to his message, it would not be necessary to follow him or anyone else. The average person off the street today may not be ready to listen. They are more content to follow. But the tide is turning. More and more people are now realizing that what or whom they are following may not be bringing them the Truth.

To Krishnamurti, following any system is the cause of all strife and warfare in the world – and one should look beyond these limited forms of belief. He discovered a way to *transcend* all belief systems and taught us how to do this. He helped us tap into the very core of our being, where the answers truly reside.

The Truth, to Krishnamurti, meant a direct insight that had to be experienced. Truth is not a theory, but provides certainty. This certainty does not and cannot come through other people. He said, "Truth does not give hope; it gives understanding.... There is no understanding in the worship of personalities." The same holds true for all other religious and political systems of the world.

If one studies Krishnamurti's teachings closely they may be found to resonate as those of a great "World Teacher." Strangely enough, maybe he *was* the World Teacher, as was prophesied, but we were not ready for him. He came by and dropped off the key. We just haven't used it yet.

Over time, his teachings have grown and can be found in more than 30 languages. Nine schools exist based entirely on his teachings, as well as 11 study centers worldwide and four Krishnamurti foundations. The American foundation in Ojai, California, is where he spent much of his time, and where he passed on in 1986. Currently, more than 150 colleges and universities are using his material worldwide. There is no doubt that his teachings will continue to be discovered and embraced during the 21st century and beyond. In the case of this particular book, we believe it to be of importance within the entire body of his work, so are therefore happy to make it available once again.